SERVING AND SURVIVING

as a human-service worker

J. Robert Russo

Southern Illinois University
Edwardsville

Waveland Press, Inc.
Prospect Heights, Illinois

To Mother

For information about this book, write or call:

Waveland Press, Inc.
P.O. Box 400
Prospect Heights, Illinois 60070
(312) 634-0081

Preface

Direct human services are projected to be the fastest growing occupations in the 1980s. It's exciting to think that you can be paid to do a job that satisfies you and makes you feel good; however, serving and surviving in bureaucratic help-giving organizations can be a real challenge. Helping is hard work. Often, your job as a human-service worker will be made more difficult by other staff members and the agency that hires you. You'll probably find that your biggest problems are not with the clients but rather with coworkers and the organization that pays you. This book is intended to help you deal with the problems caused by your coworkers and by the rules, regulations, policies, procedures, and traditions of the organization for which you work. It is designed to help those who work the longest hours, receive the lowest pay, and give the most help to clients.

As you enter your job as a human-service worker, you may bring a sense of idealism. Along with the paycheck, you hope to receive other professional and personal rewards. When such rewards don't materialize, feelings of frustration and failure develop. The prevalence of these feelings among human-service workers prompted me to write this book. It is my intention to help you put these feelings in a perspective that may make them more productive for both you and the people you serve. Some academic departments, schools, and colleges train administrators. Hundreds of books and thousands of courses are offered to help managers and bosses deal with employees and run organizations. This book is intended to help you deal with your bosses and the organization that pays you. As an employee, you justify the existence of the organization for which you work. You deliver the service and generate the records that the administration and board use to survive. You link the organization to its clients.

Many of the experiences related in this book are my own. As a client, I have been a recipient, a ward, a patient, and a student. I have worked as a gang worker, a settlement-house director, a teacher, a counselor, a professor, an administrator, a board member, and a janitor. This book is mainly an organized collection of the real-life experiences of a group of new human-service workers. Research results and other literature also are included.

If you are reading this as a textbook for a course, I hope that you, your instructor, and the other students in your class disagree, discuss, and debate as a result of what I have written. All of you will be able to provide examples that are more personal and, therefore, more meaningful than the examples I have supplied. I look forward to your comments, which can be sent to me in care of the publisher.

Many valuable suggestions were contributed by the following people, who reviewed parts or all of the original manuscript: Marlene S. Chrissinger, University of Nevada, Las Vegas; Gerald Corey, California State University, Fullerton; Barbara D'Angelo, California State University, Fullerton; Jeffrey S. Haber, Metropolitan State College, Denver, Colorado; and José George Iglesias, Pima Community College, Tucson, Arizona. The suggestions and questions of the manuscript editor, Bob Rowland, and the production editor, Trisha Cain, were genuinely helpful. Without the patience, skill, and intelligence of secretaries Gay Martin and Jackie Walker, this work would not have been possible.

J. Robert Russo

Contents

1 Introduction

All large helping institutions have much in common, though the slang may differ, the clients may differ, and problems that are minor in one institution may be major in another. This book focuses on those aspects that are common to all kinds of helping institutions. *Helping* here refers to counseling, teaching, training, educating, guiding, nursing, treating, aiding, serving, and so on. As a helping person, you will try to influence or change another person. You will expect your help to be useful and constructive. The other person will be healthier, happier, wiser, more skilled, better adjusted, or better educated as a result of your work.

Much of the material used as examples in this book was collected from taped interviews of recently hired staff members. Each of these individuals wishes to remain anonymous for reasons that will become clear as you read. The prison guards, ward attendants, teachers, counselors, psychologists, youth supervisors, nurses, and social workers relate experiences that may be of help to those of you who are beginning a career as a human-service worker. These people don't have all the answers, but their successes, as well as their mistakes, may give you hope in your career of serving others.

Job Selection, Application, and Interview

Here are a few guidelines on job selection, applications, and interviews. We really don't choose a single job from the more than 30,000 available job titles; however, we consider entering many occupations during our lives. We develop conceptions of what certain occupations involve. Our choice of jobs is based on these conceptions and the degree to which our conceptions fit our needs, desires, and talents. It is no surprise that human-service workers value working with people more than those who choose careers in business.

Initial Choices

After we select an occupational area, we choose an organization. We make such a decision at the beginning of our career. The decision is made again when we consider changing jobs. When a tight job market limits job possibilities, it may not seem as though there is much of a choice; but there is. We choose either to stay where we are or to go someplace else. When a "match up" occurs between our talent and needs and an organization's requirements and characteristics, we are confronted with a choice.

Schein (1968) has described the process of matching as the development of psychological contracts. These unwritten contracts are developed in our minds. Expectations about the attractive aspects of a new job always are included. The act of choosing seems to distort our perception. Researchers have shown that, immediately after we decide to take a new job, we tend to see it as even more attractive than we did at the time we made the choice (Lawler, Kuleck, Rhode, & Sorenson, 1975; Soelberg, 1967; Vroom, 1966). Moreover, the other alternatives that we may have been considering look much less attractive once we've made our choice. This process of justifying our choice sets us up. The letdown you may feel soon after taking a new job is at least partly related to this process of self-justification. Self-seduction and letdown seem to be common experiences among individuals beginning new careers (Vroom & Deci, 1971; Wanous, 1975; Sheridan, 1975).

Our need to justify our actions is reinforced by job recruiting and advertising practices; seldom are the less desirable elements of a job spelled out in advertisements. Even when you have heard about the job by word of mouth, each person in the information chain has added to and subtracted from the original information; the description you hear may bear little resemblance to the on-the-job situation. Simply put, you should gather as much information as possible before you make your application and begin to develop your psychological contract.

Source of Job-Related Information

Where can you obtain job-related information? Often, community college and university instructors are reliable sources of information. This can be especially true of instructors in professional schools. For example, an assessment of mental-health organizations can sometimes be made with information secured from professionals in private practice. Public agencies such as the United Way, accrediting bodies, licensing bureaus, and community referral services also can be valuable sources of information. Court administrators' offices, public defenders' staffs, and public school counselors might be "interviewed" about a job in mental health. Obtain as many answers to your questions as you can before you accept a position. I have found it useful to use a secondary source of information; that is, when I've located someone who knows about a particular job, I get the name of another person who might know something about the organization involved, and I talk to them.

Job Applications

If you decide to apply for a position, get a set of application materials. Some organizations may be willing to send them to you; others may request that you pick them up in person. If you write to the organization, the prospective employer has received the first entry in your personnel file—your letter. If you go in person, you have made your first impression. The set of application materials may range from a one-page locally developed form to a complex array of sheets, computer cards, and foldouts designed to be optically scanned and fed into a data processing system. In any case, organizations keep paper—someone will keep your application. If you are hired, your application will become a part of your personnel file, so make sure that it is neat. If your handwriting is cryptic, you should either print or have your application typed. Whatever you do, don't fill out the application hastily in the personnel office on a rough desk with a skipping ballpoint pen. Take the application home with you. Write your answers on scratch paper, and then transfer them to the application. Ask someone to read the application after you've completed it. Most prospective employers respect proper grammar, punctuation, and sentence structure. A carefully worded cover letter (typewritten) should be attached to your application. Federal and state laws restrict the type of information that a prospective employer can request on a job application. Include *relevant* additional data about yourself in your letter. Some organizations have such a poor history of open hiring and recruitment practices that they look for "triple headers"—that is, employees who can be counted three times on required government documents related to affirmative action. If you have any traits that are related to affirmative-action hiring, specify these traits in your cover letter. (Despite claims to the contrary, employers are still free to hire the most qualified applicants.)

The Interview

If you are called in for an interview, prepare for it. Most organizations consider the interview to be the most important part of the employee-selection process. From your point of view, the interview may be a tension producing event. The knowledge that an interview has been scheduled is enough to cause stomach problems for some people. If you have been scheduled for an interview, the organization has seen a set of talents and skills (yours) that might match its needs. You have already passed one screening before the interview takes place. Let's look at the pressures surrounding an interview situation. Lawler (1973, p. 100), from the University of Michigan, describes it this way:

> The organization is always faced with balancing its desire to attract the best people with its desire to gather valid selection data. The typical interview is a microcosm of these competing desires. Part of the time the interviewer is in the role of attracting the person, and part of the time he is in the role of trying to evaluate the person. This conflict can produce obvious stress and strain in the interviewer. The situation faced by the interviewer is similar to that faced by the job applicant who tries to both attract the organization and gather information about it. In a sense, deciding how to behave in the selection situation is a game played by both the organization and the job applicant, and how each one plays it depends on where he perceives he stands with respect to the other at that moment. How each one plays it also has a very strong influence on the likelihood that the selection process will result in a decision that is good for both the applicant and the organization.

Rather than let the tension build until the day and hour of the interview, you should go to work. You already know something about the organization, but you should find out more. Make sure you have at least two questions to ask the people who interview you. When the day of the interview arrives, be prompt, neat, and polite, and listen closely. *Look the interviewer in the eye at least once during the interview.* If it is a group interview, try to establish eye contact with each person in the group. Don't slouch, but try to be a little relaxed. If you feel anxious during the interview, try leaning back against the back of the chair rather than constantly sitting on the edge. It's likely that the chair you sit in will be lower than your prospective employer's chair, and a large desk will provide the interviewer with a sense of security, while you sit with nothing in front of you but your legs and feet. You may be nervous, especially if you really want the job, but remember that the interview wasn't designed to make you uncomfortable. If you are asked a question that you don't understand or can't answer, you can say "I'm not sure I understand that question. Could you ask it in a different way?" Nine times out of ten, the person who asked the question will either give you a clue to the answer or try to rephrase the question. If the interview is interrupted by a visitor or a telephone call, focus on the topic that was being discussed when the interruption occurred. As soon as the interruption is over, say something like "Before we were interrupted we were talking about . . . ."

Silence causes most people to feel uncomfortable, including the person who is interviewing you. The information questions that you had planned before the interview can be used during any uncomfortable pauses. The questions you plan in advance can serve two purposes. Planned questions can fill in silence and, at the same time, allow you to interview the interviewer. Questions that relate to something that was said earlier in the interview indicate your ability to listen and recall. The following is an example of such a question: "Earlier you said you had worked here for five years. What major attributes of this organization attracted you during that period?" Planned questions can help you to determine the philosophy of helping held by an organization or by the people who are interviewing you. A question such as "What are the major strengths of your clients?" may elicit responses varying from shock to a description of an agency's philosophy.

When you are asked "Is there anything else you want to say?" you should ask your heaviest question, if you haven't already used it. Examples of heavy questions are: "What would you judge to be the major two or three problems that your organization now faces?" or "What do you see as the major changes that need to be made to improve the organization's service?"

The First Three Months

Often, new workers are frantic workers. They are impatient. They forget that the process of growing, learning, healing—changing in any way—is both complex and natural. You took the job as a human-service worker to help people through this process. You will soon discover that most of your coworkers don't seem to feel the same way you do. Before you make harsh judgments of more experienced workers, and before you begin to give your clients all you've got, use some of your energy to get to know the organization for which you work. Hoffer (1967, p. 4), the longshoreman turned professor, says that workers who are sure of their skills go leisurely about their jobs and accomplish much; they work as though they are at play. Many individuals beginning careers in human services attack their work as though they were saving the world. Remember, your clients had their needs before you arrived.

The Organization's Norms

You can get to know an organization by becoming familiar with its norms. *Norms* are unwritten rules and guidelines that are understood and followed by the members of a group. Student nurses are taught that the patient-care plan is a carefully conceived, well-written document that should be developed by all of the staff members on the floor. They are told that the plan should provide the basis for conferences in which the staff members discuss each of the patients. However, most hospitals don't follow this procedure. Some schools contain more than one teachers' lounge; one of the lounges may be for a selected group of faculty members. In a public health clinic, the physical exams may not include blood samples, even though these are required by the federal government. In a mental hospital, TV programs may be selected by the patients according to formal rules; however, a complex system may exist whereby staff members bribe selected patients to tune in the programs that the staff wants to watch. Working in a prison, guards may discover that, regardless of the situation, they should never accept lights from inmates, because that gesture is associated with bribery. You may find out that, even when the supervisor's office door is open, you are expected to knock before you enter. These practices and rules are all examples of norms. The more norms you can identify in an organization, the more productive and satisfied you will be in that organization. How many reports, observations, lesson plans, tickets, or memos are you expected to complete each week? Do the other workers fall behind in their work, or do they stay late or come early to see clients, to catch up, and to complete paperwork?

Even though you want to prove to everyone that you are a competent, hardworking employee, you should find out what is considered an acceptable work rate before you give it all you've got. A new employee is not usually punished for being too slow. The organization that hired you expects that it will take time for you to learn your job. Moreover, experienced employees may "punish" you if you unknowingly "break the rate." After you've learned what the work rate is, you'll have a chance to make a choice (rather than violate an important norm by accident). You can then ask yourself "Do I go along with the norm, or am I going to behave differently?" This question is one that you will have to face as long as you work in a human organization.

Conflict between You and the Norms

You know what is right for yourself. You've been trained, schooled, and educated, and you know how to do your job. The difference between what you know should be and what you really find will cause many conflicts.

Here, an established employee (a security guard) describes one early experience:

> We had what we called *lock up*. Whenever there was something going on, the kids were locked in their rooms. This was the rule that the superintendent thought was a must—the way you should deal with kids who are to be locked up from the courts. I didn't really think too much of that rule. It created a lot of dissension between me and the kids. It really made a lot of work for me, and I kinda rebelled against that. But I managed to find other ways to get kids out—from being locked up. I always had some kind of a job or cleanup—something for the kids to do that I could use to keep them out of their rooms. I had a heck of a lot more cooperation from the kids. I did not have the fighting, confusion, broken windows, ripped up toilet stools, and that kind of stuff. Before long, I had what looked like a happy group of kids in our wing. The other guys [security men] couldn't quite really understand or figure out what I was doing—why I had such a quiet wing. I was called on the carpet a couple of times about how come my boys were always out when they should have been locked up. Each time, I told them that my kids had work to do. This seemed to satisfy my supervisors; it hadn't created any security risk, and it did keep things quiet. The other guys working with me saw what was happening. They had a hard time buying it, because they were strictly "lock up and forget it." Finally, they realized that, if they let the kids out and kept them busy, they could have a quiet wing too and an easier day for themselves as well as for the kids. I think I better elaborate a little more on this. I think I better tell you about "bending the rules." If you feel you have to put a little kink in a rule, you just don't kink it to kink it; you'd better evaluate it and look at it closely when you finally decide

that you are going to bend it. You have to use good judgment and common sense. I really got lucky on this one.

An example of a conflict between established rules and the behavior of coworkers is described in the following anecdote. This employee had been placed on the night shift as the lone attendant in a security tower, where he was armed with a rifle.

> During the first month or so in the tower, the lieutenant constantly called me up and wanted to know what was going on. He was really checking to see whether I was awake. As part of his nightly duties, he would go to the far corner of the yard to feed the dogs twice a night. It was an institution rule that any employee who was in the yard at night would flash a light, and I was to flash an acknowledgment. He was then to flash me back. I would flash him and he wouldn't flash me in return. This happened for about two or three days, and I finally said the heck with it. I didn't flash him. Then he began to flash me. I would flash him back, but he wouldn't flash me back. This happened for a couple of days; then he proceeded in the same way—he would not flash. I would flash and he wouldn't acknowledge. Then it got to the point where I wouldn't flash and he would call me up and want to know if I was awake. He told me to stay with it, or else. So one night I decided there had to be something done in order to change this man's attitude. I knew he was coming down to feed the dogs at an approximate time. I unloaded the 30-30, and I waited for him to come into sight. It was about 4:00 A.M.   I remember the night air was real still. As he came around the corner to feed the dogs, I flashed him. He didn't flash me in any way, or acknowledge in any way, so I opened the door to the tower, stepped out on the ledge, lifted the bolt on the rifle, put the flashlight on the barrel, and pointed it in the direction of the dogs. The hammer clicked in the night air. He flashed me immediately, and, from that point on, he called me up every time to let me know he was going down to feed the dogs.

Conflicts can be seen as opportunities to change and grow, to bargain and reconcile, and to compete and mediate. Before you tackle the resolution of any conflict, you should consider two major items: (1) a set of priorities and (2) a personal-support system. Priorities may be listed in several ways. One list might reflect the degree of difficulty; another might indicate how long it will take to resolve each conflict; a third might detail the "actors," their positions in the organization, and their relationships to one another. (You can think of this last list as a limited sociogram.) A final list could rank conflicts according to their importance to you. Your task is to combine these lists. It is not unusual to discover that the various lists interlock. The conflicts that you have identified will most likely form a web. It is not usually possible to tackle one conflict without becoming involved with the others.

After you've made some *tentative* choices about where you should begin, consider your personal-support systems. What resources will you need? Are those resources available to you? One of your most important resources will be the psychological support of your coworkers. A spouse, a friend, or a roommate can provide a viewpoint that you have not considered. Those who value and respect you and your skills become even more important when the going gets rough.

Conflicts are not resolved quickly and easily. Conflict only occurs in the context of interdependence. In other words, you and the things that are causing you trouble are dependent on each other to some extent—otherwise, there would be no conflict. You might be tempted to isolate yourself from "them" or "it." The results of such a strategy of isolation are most likely visible in your organization. Poor communication is only one negative result of isolation. More damaging to the organization in the long run is that supervisors may see the absence of conflict as a sign that cooperation is taking place. In terms of service delivery, such an assumption can be damaging to both the staff and the clients. Isolation postpones the resolution of conflicts and often acts to magnify the original problems. The solution of most human problems takes time. You have to keep working, even though you may be working in a less-than-ideal situation. A former student of mine puts it this way:

> As I began my job in a training school for the mentally handicapped, I realized that all of the 500 residents needed some sort of help. Fresh out of college and full of ideas, I really felt that I could help in making some changes in their lives. Then the "system" became evident to me, and the frustration of not being able to make progress became overwhelming. Everything I started became bogged down with paperwork, policies, and apathetic coworkers. It soon occurred to me that attempting to change the entire setup was unrealistic. So, I began to single out specific residents with specific problems and concentrated my efforts on them. I was then told by my supervisors and coworkers that I was playing favorites. But, by channeling my efforts on one resident at a time, I could actually see some positive results over a period of time. When one child learned to walk alone, or learned to feed himself, or was placed in a home setting, all the hassle was worthwhile.

Some conflicts may seem simple; make sure you have all the information you need before you attempt to find resolutions. For example, it is foolish to criticize an established employee before you know all of the details. Genuine compliments are usually accepted by coworkers. Questions asked of carefully selected coworkers usually are answered. Most staff members with whom I've worked—especially teachers—don't go up the line for help; they ask other staff members at the same level. Being a student or trainee yesterday and a staff member today can be a shock. You may not be sure whether you'll sink or swim. Some of the other staff members at your level have had years of experience. They may share some of their experience with you, but don't be too surprised if some established employees give you the sink-or-swim response. A new prison guard had this experience:

> I can recall the first night I worked the yard detail. I had an officer—an old officer who had been there approximately 15 years—and, as we started the yard trip for the clock run, I told the officer that I was new on the assignment and that he would have to explain where we were going and what we were doing. He told me I would learn the same way he did. Nobody told him, and he wasn't about to tell me. And so that was the way it was. I just watched, and when it came time for my turn to take the yard watch by myself, I just had to play it by ear.

Your clients are subject to norms. In many ways, they have a more difficult job than you do in discovering unwritten rules. High school students quickly learn formal rules. They learn that they must walk up the "up" staircases and down the "down" staircases. They must not run in the halls. They must not be late to classes. They even learn complex traffic patterns, such as the changing one-way directions of certain hallways during certain times of the day. At the same time, the students learn informal laws, or norms. For example, they must not cut in front of a teacher in the lunch line or smoke in certain areas. These kinds of norms are relatively easy to learn. There is a more complex set of norms that depend on the particular staff person involved. Don't call a teacher by his or her first name when that teacher, or another teacher, can hear you. The school rule specifies that students are not to be tardy to class. The students quickly learn, however, that some teachers allow a 30-second leniency before they count a student as tardy. Some teachers always allow a few minutes near the end of the class period for talking or studying. Some teachers do not give homework over weekends and holidays. Usually, teachers who establish these kinds of norms (which are understood by the student) expect something in return, such as good behavior when a supervisor is in the room or when a substitute teacher takes over the class. These kinds of "contracts" between staff and clients are discovered slowly and are never discussed openly. The skillfulness with which we can discern these contracts is a tribute to human ingenuity. Perceptive clients quickly learn whether or not you are the kind of person with whom they can crack a joke and under what conditions you will accept and approve of this kind of behavior. Clients learn, for instance, that they can trade jokes with you only when there are no other staff members present. Smith (1968) observed a teacher, Bill Geoffrey, for nearly one year and wrote a fascinating book describing his observations. Licata and Willower (1975) have studied student brinkmanship—that is, the art of driving teachers crazy without getting into trouble. The testing of authority is familiar to any of us who have ever sat in a classroom. The skill level of the clients determines how sophisticated this testing becomes. In the late 1930s, Hayner and Ash (1939) conducted one of the first studies on prison inmates. They describe the complex process of producing *jo* (coffee) in prison cells. They conclude this description by saying "The successful evasion of a rule is even more satisfying than the finished product" (p. 362). The process by which clients find out what makes you tick is very complex and systematic; the outcome of that process will, in part, determine how effective you are on your job.

As you read Chapter 2, you will see that generations of human-service workers have fought the good fight and made some significant improvements. Still, much needs to be done. Nurses discover that they cannot do the kind of nursing for which they were trained because of the very large patient/nurse ratio: "When you come out and you're the R.N., you're probably put in as a charge nurse and you simply just don't have the time to give the total patient care that you were taught." A beginning teacher is torn between the desire to change the outdated methods and attitudes toward education and the need for the department chairperson's approval.

Feedback

After a few weeks, you'll probably wonder how you're doing on the job. No one has really told you. You may begin to feel that you're not doing well, because nobody has said anything about your work. You need reliable feedback in order to evaluate yourself and your performance. Sometimes a straight question addressed to your supervisor will elicit a straight answer. Carefully chosen coworkers may be one source of feedback; but staff members may not tell you what you want to know.

You may have found a coworker you can really trust. Perhaps an established worker who wants to help you will give you a Dutch Uncle Talk—that is, something like "What really counts around here are the papers in your file—not the service you give to the clients. The promotions, the raises, and the vacation time come from the bureaucracy in the organization, not from the clients. We do it this way here." The purpose of such a talk is to make you face the fact that your expectations and personal values are not the expectations and values of the organization for which you work. If, after being confronted with this point of view, you are still in the revolutionary and paranoid stage, more drastic action may be taken. A psychiatric aide had this experience:

> The patients' luncheon used to come on food elevators, and I was one of the people who were to pick them out, prepare to serve them, and then serve them after the patients came to pick their food. There were usually two or three other psychiatric aides besides me. Most of the food that was for the patients was awfully big pieces. The food would come up, and they would line up, and we would have to serve them one by one. One of the first shocking things that I was asked to do was to throw away about 15 uneaten hamburgers and open three or four quarts of unopened milk cartons and throw them all in the garbage disposal. Having come from a starving nation, I was really shocked. I protested, but the nursing supervisor told me that there was no point in sending the food down, because this would mean more of a problem for the kitchen people, who would then have to store the food back. And so I had better throw all of these uneaten hamburgers and unopened cartons of milk in the garbage disposal. Once, I did return some of those milk cartons back to the kitchen only to find at the next meal they did not send any milk up.

Humor and sarcasm often are used to tell newcomers that they have messed up, or violated a norm. A secondary-school teacher reports these incidents:

> My first year I was really gung-ho with my room. I tried to decorate the bulletin boards and make displays. Well, people thought this was hilarious. They kept telling me that I should go and teach second grade if I liked doing this. I did it anyway. One day I just decided I had enough. Someone stuck their head in and said something very sarcastic. I said "If more people around here would decorate their rooms, the kids might be more willing to come and sit in that class for an hour and a half." I needed help that first year. I didn't need someone to come in and laugh at me.

Adjustment to Failure

Adjustment to failure is a central part of a new employee's socialization process. This adjustment is difficult, because the new employee is usually fired up with spirit and idealism. After all, you have been successful throughout your educational career and, more often than not, have a firm desire to be humanistic, concerned, and considerate to all your clients. Moreover, your internship has probably been successful. Consequently, when a client fails to respond to your efforts, you experience a sense of failure. The following poem describes the feelings of a beginning English teacher:

> The school room is dark, and a womb that knows no birth
> But dies and dies again, no birth, no life to give
> To John or Jane. A factual facade
> Caresses tight and lets no living in.
> The teacher only lives a dream of know.
> He hides behind the is or cannot be
> And fails to hear and see the I and me
> That sits behind the silent crying eyes.
>
> But sometimes when the sun cracks through those stones
> That keep the touch of outside from the in
> The radiant hopes of sunshine kisses warm
> Despite a touch of maybe through the walls.
> And golden raindrops smooth and soft and sheer
> Caress and free those dreams that still may live.

Summary

Perhaps you have a job that involves helping people; or, maybe you are considering such a job. In this chapter, guidelines are offered on job selection, application, and interview behavior. Maybe you'll apply and be interviewed. If a "match up" occurs between your talents and needs and an organization's requirements, you'll take the job and work with a group of employees. Since the day you entered kindergarten, you have been a newcomer to groups. You have experienced the tension before; but, somehow this is different now. The work situation probably won't turn out to be quite what you expected it to be.

Helping is hard work. Once you've been trained to help clients, your biggest problems will be with your coworkers and the rules, regulations, policies, procedures, and traditions of the organization for which you work.

Your job environment contains dedicated staff members, helpful supervisors, and appreciative clients. If you focus too much energy on the negative aspects of your workplace, you may lack the energy you need to do your job and maintain your own mental and physical health. Your mental health and professional responsibilities require you to maintain a balance.

Discussion Questions

1. What is your personal-support system? Whom do you go to for help?
2. What physical place or places in your life feel most comfortable to you?
3. What are the norms that operate in your classroom or present work situation? For example, for the former, make a list of norms regarding attendance, verbal participation, and relationships with instructors. For the latter, describe the norms associated with work rate, coffee or other refreshment use, the staff lounge area, dress codes, and so on.
4. Which of these norms are nonproductive? How could you change them?
5. Name several philosophies of helping. Describe the assumptions about clients inherent in each of these philosophies.
6. Describe your philosophy of helping.

References

Hayner, N. S., & Ash, E. The prisoner community as a social group. *American Sociological Review*, 1939, *4*, 362-369.

Hoffer, E. *The ordeal of change.* New York: Harper & Row, 1967.

Lawler, E. E., III. *Motivation in work organizations.* Monterey, Calif.: Brooks/ Cole, 1973.

Lawler, E. E., III, Kuleck, W. J., Rhode, J. G., & Sorenson, J. E. Job choice and post decision dissonance. *Organizational Behavior and Human Performance*, 1975, *13*, 133-145.

Licata, J. W., & Willower, D. J. Student brinkmanship and the school as a social system. *Educational Administration Quarterly*, Spring 1975, *9*(2), 1-14.

Schein, E. H. Organizational socialization and the profession of management. *Industrial Management Review*, 1968, *9*, 1-16.

Sheridan, J. E., Richards, M. D., & Slocom, J. W. Comparative analysis of expectancy and heuristic models of decision behavior. *Journal of Applied Psychology*, 1975, *60*, 361-368.

Smith, L. M., & Geoffrey, W. *The complexities of an urban classroom: An analysis toward a general theory of teaching.* New York: Holt, Rinehart & Winston, 1968.

Soelberg, P. Unprogrammed decision making. *Industrial Management Review*, 1967, *8*, 19-29.

Vroom, V. H. Organizational choice: A study of the pre and post decision process. *Organizational Behavior and Human Performance*, 1966, *1*, 212-225.

Vroom, V. H., & Deci, E. L. The stability of post decisional dissonance: A follow-up study of job attitude of business school graduates. *Organizational Behavior and Human Performance*, 1971, *6*, 36-49.

Wanous, J. P. *Organizational entry: The transition from outsider to newcomer to insider.* Working paper 75-14. New York University, Graduate School of Business Administration, 1975.

2 The Roots of Bureaucratic Help Giving

Introduction

Human-service institutions and organizations have emerged through a historical process. This chapter examines the evolution of our present human-services system.[1] The information provided here may help you to become a more effective help giver and change agent. History can provide a perspective on the present and help to predict the near future.

This is a great and yet frightening time. Interplanetary technology, electronic wonders of the media, genetic engineering, political scandals, pollution, inflation, and rapidly changing cultural values are typical of the events and developments that confuse intelligent people (Brennecke & Amick, 1975). The quiet desperation that Thoreau saw as the basis of life for the masses was only a ripple on Walden Pond when compared with the torrent of confusion today.

Some individuals find comfort in believing that the meaning and purpose of their lives are written in the stars. Perhaps it is well to have such beliefs; if we search history for life's meaning, we come up short! Despite the efforts of generations of social workers, priests, teachers, and governments, tens of thousands of people still sleep in the streets of Calcutta and Karachi. Sewage contaminates the drinking water of Lagos. Children in Brazil are

[1]The author is grateful to Judith Cingolani, M.S.W., Department of Sociology and Social Work, Southern Illinois University at Edwardsville, for her helpful suggestions during the preparation of this chapter.

abandoned by the thousands, because their parents cannot afford to feed them (Walsh, 1969). The great thinkers do not agree as to the nature and purpose of humanity. To remind ourselves of our own special place, we can recount great deeds performed in the past; however, historians find it difficult to discover one deed— no matter how important that deed was to a particular time and place—that permanently affects the future. Great deeds do, however, provide examples of solutions to be modified and improved. This is your challenge. As you read this history of human-service organizations, try to determine where you are going to fit and what you are going to improve.

If you have chosen to spend a part of your life as a help giver, a brief look at some historical roots may be an aid to you in maintaining a balance between the psychological and professional responsibilities that you may face in your job.

As social animals, human beings are dependent on one another. If we are going to talk about improving social functioning and minimizing pain, we must look at social structure. Our dependence on others can be a source of great satisfaction as well as the cause of great suffering. Suffering has always been a result of a breakdown of the social network. By banding together, we have attempted to ensure our basic survival, protection, and reproduction. Beyond that, human groups make possible the highly complex social patterns in which we live. The first human group was possibly the family, which reflected sexuality and the need for protection. The family was the first social-welfare unit. There are those who claim that the family is the dominant unit in our culture today. Originally, the family was the only social-welfare unit, but recently it has been supplemented by other social structures. Today we have a complex network of help-giving organizations and institutions (Federico, 1976).

In reading this chapter, it may help you to have a conceptual framework. Throughout history, people have dealt with two basic problem areas—dependency and deviancy, or "dangerous" behavior. The reactions to these two basic problems and their solutions have depended on the prevailing beliefs of the time. There are three major beliefs regarding the causes of dependency and deviancy; each belief corresponds to a parallel solution. If God, fate, or nature is the cause, the solution is "relief money," punishment, or acceptance without action. If the individual is at fault, the solution is to either change (rehabilitate) the person or remove him or her from society. If the system is at fault, social engineering is the solution. As you will see later in this chapter, governments respond in several ways to these problems. (Since the knowledge and technology needed to apply social engineering are just beginning to emerge, government use of social engineering has been less than effective.)

In looking at the past, many actions may seem inhumane to us. Remember, brutality may have been present simply because people were ignorant—they didn't know what else to do. They saw the situation differently than we do today. They no doubt saw the gap between the real and the ideal much as we do. Years from now, our professional progeny may view us as stupid and inept as they view the world and apply their new knowledge to old problems.

The Colonial Period

This brief history of human-service organizations begins with the colonial period in the United States. Poverty and crime in the 18th century were not seen as indications of defects in community organization; they were accepted as natural phenomena. Poverty was tolerated by the prevailing religious teachings. The definition of the term *poor* covered a wide variety of individuals, including widows, orphans, the sick, the insane, and the physically disabled. The critical element in the definition was not the cause of poverty, but rather the fact that certain individuals were needy. The condition of poverty was accepted; this acceptance was encouraged by the clergy. In fact, the presence of poor people provided an opportunity for well-to-do individuals to exercise Christian virtue in the form of stewardship. The rich could do good by giving to the poor (Rothman, 1971).

As long as there was a need in the economy for unskilled and uneducated workers, universal public education seemed inappropriate. Under these conditions, noninstitutional mechanisms of relief, education, and corrections seemed logical and appropriate to the colonists.

During the colonial period, criminals were handled quite directly. As early as 1662, every county in Virginia was ordered to construct stocks and a whipping post. The stocks symbolized the colonial notion of a self-policing community. Punishment in the stocks involved discomfort, but not physical pain. If physical punishment had been the colonists' goal, they would have relied exclusively on the whip. The use of stocks operated in a more powerful way. Offenders were held up to public ridicule—an extreme punishment and an important deterrent in closely knit communities. More extreme measures were occasionally taken, such as driving offenders through town in a cart and whipping them.

These punishments sometimes included a branding that signified the offense. Branding was certainly painful, but it also had a Cain-and-Abel quality about it. This was effective social control of citizens who were concerned about their neighbors' reactions. As long as people lived in closely knit communities with very few transients, such a system operated quite well. Some larger communities found it necessary to construct a special room on public property to house the "extremely insane"—those who had become too disruptive. Part of the severity of the early colonial period resulted from the fact that little communities survived their formative years by depending on everyone to be productive and pull together; nonproductiveness and deviance were seen as threats to the delicate and precarious social fabric.

As the population grew and people began to move about, each colony enacted laws that denied relief to the transient poor. These laws included penalties for citizens who housed needy people without notifying the proper officials. Transient poor were to be escorted to the edge of the community and expelled. During this era, debate was focused on the effectiveness of giving help to those who needed it. It was clear that widows, orphans, and the physically impaired were incapable of supporting themselves. When the numbers of such worthy poor became too large to be housed in private residences, the institution of the almshouse emerged; it quickly came to be known as the poorhouse—one of the earliest forms of "indoor relief." Needy persons were taken in and helped. The almshouses soon became a repository not only for the poor but also for deviants, including the mentally ill, whom the community was unable to house in private residences.

Almshouses, or poorhouses, were operated by nongovernmental agencies. Churches and other volunteer organizations were responsible for these institutions as well as a majority of other health and welfare functions. Public responsibility for such activities evolved very slowly, due to the stewardship of the rich and the acceptance of the biblical claim that the poor will always be with us (Gilbert & Specht, 1976).

The impact of ministers and religious organizations on the treatment of criminals was very direct; they placed little faith in the possibility of reform and rehabilitation. The prevailing Calvinist beliefs emphasized the natural depravity of humanity; according to these beliefs, rehabilitation would be a waste of time. In addition, local officials believed that the best protection against recidivism was eviction of offenders from the community.

During the colonial period, punishment was closely related to "an eye for an eye and a tooth for a tooth" doctrine. This general motive of revenge reflected religious doctrines. In the late 1700s, the Society of Friends, or the Quakers, took a lead in bringing about a shift in attitude from punishment to rehabilitation. The transformation of attitudes from corporal punishment to imprisonment occurred as a rise in moralist notions regarding crime and criminals took place.

Colonial Prison Systems

During this period, jails housed both criminals and the insane. The justification of imprisonment was based on deterrence. The Quakers felt that the theory of punishment as a deterrent was related to the motive of revenge. As it turned out, the prison discipline was probably as brutal as earlier corporal punishment. The new brutality took place behind prison walls, well removed from the public. This isolation effectively removed whatever deterrent influence the earlier community discipline might have exercised; nonetheless, prisons were constructed and systems of discipline were implemented.

The first U.S. prison was built in Philadelphia around 1800. This prison, which came to be known as the Pennsylvania system, enforced separate confinement and absolute silence. The construction of such a prison involved a great deal of expense, and separate confinement and total silence were not well adapted to many prison industries. As a result, an alternative system was developed 25 years later in Auburn, New York. In the Auburn system, prisoners were confined in solitude during the night, but they were allowed to work together in shops during the day. Since complete silence was imposed on the prisoners when they were outside their cells, the Auburn system became silent and solitary. These prisons were visited by individuals from many countries; some saw them as ideal models. The Auburn system became popular in the U.S., whereas the Pennsylvania system was widely adopted abroad.

The Elmira Reformatory

Both the Pennsylvania and Auburn prison systems were notorious failures in reforming or rehabilitating criminals. Their failure contributed to the development of the Elmira Reformatory—an adaptation of the Irish prison system, which was based on the indeterminate sentence and provided that release be based on conduct in the institution. The Elmira Reformatory opened in 1876. Although it was a great advance over the old Pennsylvania and Auburn systems, it was applied only to first offenders between the ages of 16 and 30.

Early in the 20th century, and continuing well after World War I, considerable effort was made in the U.S. to introduce the Elmira ideals of reform into traditional prisons. Classification systems that separated prisoners on the basis of various treatments were widely recommended and were tried in some cases. The physical structures used for prisons became more humane and more attractive. The basic philosophy in the practices of the traditional system remained; the reform program was frustrated by the fact that the criminal law was focused on composing a fitting punishment for a given crime.

The Establishment of Mental Hospitals

In the 1830s, Horace Mann, to whom I will refer later, made a special plea for the separation of the insane from criminals. His plea to the Massachusetts legislature was partly a result of a report describing the horrible conditions in the Dedham House of Corrections, which, at that time, housed criminals as well as the insane. A report submitted by George Burrows maintained that 40% of all mental patients in a group of European hospitals had recovered (cited in Messerli, 1972). Francis Willis claimed that 90% of all mental patients could recover, if they received treatment within three months of their first attack (cited in Messerli, 1972). Mann's plea included the claim that local communities had given up their responsibility for the care of the insane to the state by default. He described the results of this default in horrible detail. For example, he pointed out that some individuals who were judged to be insane were imprisoned in basement rooms for 20 years. They slept on beds of straw and were given their food through slots. As a result of Mann's pleas, a state mental hospital was established (Messerli, 1972).

Mann developed what appears to be the first classification system for clients in mental hospitals. The first category included "lunatics whose freedom threatened the public welfare." Clients in this category were clearly the responsibility of the state. Clients in the second category were both lunatics and town paupers. These individuals were the responsibility of their local communities. Often, the services of these people were auctioned to the highest bidder, who would then put them to work as payment for their room and board. Members of the third category were neither the charge of the state nor of the town, because they constituted no threat to the public welfare. They were admitted to the hospital when payment was received from their families or friends.

When the Worcester State Lunatic Hospital opened in 1833,

Massachusetts Governor Levy Lincoln issued a call for the reception of the insane into the institution:

> Across the state from jails and houses of correction of every county, the lunatics were prepared for transfer. Amidst oaths, obscene language, and a general chorus of demented cacophony, the products of years of neglect were led or forced from their stenchladen cellars, cages, and closets. Coming into the daylight, they could be seen in all their disfigured hideousness—the fierce testimony of the ravages of filth, anguish, and barbarism. As the jailors cut off their garments stinking with sweat and urine, scrubbed their bodies with strong soap, and dressed them in new clothes, they could not be expected to comprehend that they, who had been forgotten by one generation, now had been singled out as the objects of intense hope by the next. Within their new home, they were to become the living demonstration of what could be accomplished through humane and enlightened methods. In place of restraint, exposure, and cruelty were to be substituted sanitation, love, and understanding, as the aspirations of humanitarian reform were to be put to a test on the outcome. It was a time when men believed the deaf could be taught to "hear," the dumb to "talk," and the blind to "see" [Messerli, 1972, p. 135].[2]

Paralleling the work and concerns of Horace Mann was Dorothea Dix, who (quite by accident) visited a jail in East Cambridge, Massachusetts, in 1841 and was shocked at the treatment received by the insane inmates. As a result of her relentless campaign of letter writing and speaking, great improvements in the treatment of the insane were accomplished. In addition, her efforts influenced the operation of jails and almshouses. She placed significant emphasis on an attempt to rehabilitate for the purpose of returning the dependents to their families and society as quickly as possible.

The New England Institute for the Education of the Blind

In order to demonstrate that human will and enlightenment could triumph over the obstacles that had been deemed impossible for centuries, the New England Institute for the Education of the Blind was opened in 1790. Horace Mann was appointed as a trustee of this institution. The blind, like the insane, were thought to be susceptible to great progress and intellectual and moral development with appropriate treatment. The superintendent of this institution, Samuel Howe, experimented with string soaked in

---

[2] From *Horace Mann: A Biography*, by J. Messerli. Copyright 1972 by Alfred A. Knopf, Inc. Reprinted by permission.

glue to produce raised images of the letters of the alphabet and maps. These attempts to teach the blind to "see" by touch appear to have been the beginning of an early system of Braille.

Horace Mann

In 1837, Mann was appointed as the first secretary of the State Board of Education for Massachusetts. Since he had become known as an outstanding public speaker, he was invited to present the Fourth of July address in Worcester County. Messerli (1972) comments on this address:

> To those citizens concerned about the future of the nation, he depicted the common schools as the necessary foundation of republican government; to worried parents, he described the schoolteacher as their partner in accomplishing what neither could do alone; to the anxious working man, he spoke of education as the great equalizer and the "creator of wealth undreamed of"; to the religious, he held up the common school as the only agency capable of moral education in an age of endemic sectarianism; and he assured the wealthy, whose property taxes were to bear most of the burden in financing the schools, that only educated children would grow up to respect their property. In an emerging industrial society, where the older paths to economic success could no longer be traveled, the public school was the best means for maintaining an equality of opportunity. Furthermore, as the ballot was increasingly extended to the rank-and-file citizen, education was the only means for providing a literate electorate essential to representative government. And finally, as other agencies seemed unable to fulfill their traditional responsibilities, the public school must come to their aid. Basically, however, its function was neither economical nor political, but moral. As Mann summed up his points, he insisted that the ultimate object and end of public education was "to form character" [pp. 263–264].

Mann is probably best known for his contributions to public education. In addition to his development of the common, or public, school movement, he initiated state teachers' colleges, originally known as Normal Schools. However, somewhat of a backlash to the state control of public education developed in Massachusetts between 1840 and 1855. State control of the curriculum produced some serious concerns and led to the movement toward local control of public schools. Until the massive federal intervention of the past several decades, local control continued as the dominant form of governance for public education in the U.S. Mann had significant impact on other social institutions, including mental hospitals, jails, and special schools for the blind. He was also instrumental in civil rights activities. In cooperation with a young attorney, Roger Baldwin, Mann represented a group of men who had taken over a slave ship in 1840. Mann and Baldwin successfully defended the case, and the potential slaves were returned to their homeland. Mann also participated in the defense of a White, Washington, D.C., shipowner who apparently had contrived to help a group of slaves to escape.

European Roots

As we have seen, the roots of current bureaucratic help giving reach far into the past. Even though we have focused primarily on its beginnings in the United States, several significant changes in Europe were particularly important in setting the stage and patterns for the development of institutions and agencies in the U.S. In 1536, a law was passed in England directing local authorities and churches to collect funds to support the poor. This legislative act was an attempt to do away with the extremely repressive measures taken against the poor and the needy. The law also made public begging illegal. Details for the accounting of money collected and distributed were included. Funds were to be given to individuals who were poor, sick, impotent, diseased, or unable to work. This law is significant, because it marked a shift in England from completely voluntary help giving to a state-run and directed human-service system. During the following seven decades, few changes were made in this early English poor law. However, during the reign of Queen Elizabeth, a series of laws were enacted that have come to be designated as the Elizabethan Poor Laws. The Act of 1601 described three classes of individuals to be helped: (1) the able-bodied poor, who were to be provided either with jobs or with punishment in prison or stocks if they refused to accept employment; (2) the impotent poor, who were to be kept in almshouses; and (3) dependent children, who were to be apprenticed, unless their parents or grandparents could take care of them. The girls were held in an apprenticeship until the age of 21, or until they married. The boys were to be apprentices until they were 24. These Elizabethan Poor Laws provided the primary basis for social welfare in England for more than 200 years. This model was largely adopted by the colonists in the U.S.

In 1834, a new law in England divided the country into districts, each of which was controlled and directed by salaried government officers. Each officer was authorized to build at least one workhouse. All support for able-bodied persons outside the workhouses was abolished. This government intervention in England, however, did not mark the end of private charities. Instead of direct relief, these charities began to focus their concern on social reform.

During the U.S. colonial period, the basic pattern for assisting the poor, the homeless, and other unfortunate types followed the laws and the activities of England very closely. As we have seen, small towns and local governments provided services that were very similar to those provided in England. Almshouses were established as a means of indoor relief. Initially, outdoor relief was administered to the poor in their own homes. The colonists expanded the concept of the placement or boarding of dependents to include both children and adults. Orphaned or neglected children and disabled individuals were auctioned to the highest bidder, who would care for them in return for their labor. The debate over the effectiveness of removing neglected children from their homes, the placement of children in alternative or foster homes, or caring for these children in state-run institutions continues to this day. Each new article or study that focuses on the subject stirs up new arguments. Before 1900, the director of the Boston Children's Aid Society suggested that each case should be treated as unique and that the placement alternative should suit the needs of the individual (Kamerman & Kahn, 1976). Since the mid-1960s, the position that each child should be treated individually has forced most children's institutions away from the custodial model.

Public Health and Welfare

The beginning of the child-welfare movement in the U.S. could be determined by a variety of events. In 1729, an orphanage was established in New Orleans for the children of those who had been victims of a massacre. In 1790, an orphanage was opened in Charleston, South Carolina, along with Mann's school for the blind in Massachusetts. A school for the "deaf and dumb" was opened in Connecticut in 1817.

As early as 1798, the federal government had established the Marine Hospital Service to provide health benefits for neglected merchant seamen. These seamen were often put ashore because they were unable to perform the jobs for which they had been hired. The first hospital to be built under the auspices of the government program was located at Fort Independence, Massachusetts; its construction marks the beginning of the public-health service in the U.S. An immediate motive for its construction was to allay the threat of a smallpox epidemic that could have been set off by merchant seamen infected in foreign ports and returning to the United States.

In 1827, President John Quincy Adams set up a payroll-deduction plan to finance the Public-Health Service. Shipowners were required to deduct 20¢ per month from each sailor aboard ship. Soon, the program was extended to cover every officer and sailor in the U.S. Navy. Within 100 years, the service was expanded to include a network of hospitals and other facilities. However, it was not until 1867 that the Department of the Interior and the Office of Education were created. Initially, these offices were limited to gathering and disseminating facts about public education and literacy rates. Until 1930, the primary motivation for the continuation of these government-funded human-service programs was charity. Pressure from organizations such as the National Consumers League and the Child Labor Committee provided the impetus for these programs. By 1912, the federal government had established the Children's Bureau; the Public-Health Service became part of the Department of the Treasury. In 1923, President Harding proposed the creation of the Department of Education and Welfare; this department, of course, is what we now know as Health, Education, and Welfare.

An Early Echo of More Need than Available Service

The depression that followed the U.S. Civil War produced family, personal, and community problems that had no precedents. These problems led to increased government involvement in providing human services. Moreover, the depression stimulated the development of voluntary charity organizations that were patterned after those in Europe. It quickly became apparent that numerous private agencies and community welfare councils needed to be coordinated, especially in heavily populated areas. The first such coordination appears to have taken place in Buffalo, New York in 1877. Similar coordinating agencies were soon developed in all large population centers. In 1909, Pittsburgh and Milwaukee established councils, or social agencies. This attempt at coordination had been preceded by the establishment of a community-wide effort to collect funds for the support of voluntary agencies. The first fund-raising effort was conducted in Denver in 1887. In 1950, more than 1400 voluntary agencies existed in the U.S. In 1978, the number had grown to 2300.

Settlement Houses

A brief history of social and welfare services in the United States would be incomplete without a discussion of the development of settlement houses. These were neighborhood centers in large urban areas that attempted to meet the recreational, health, and welfare needs of all residents. There were several pioneers in the settlement-house movement. The first settlement house was organized in 1886 in New York. Three years later, Jane Addams established Hull House in Chicago. Addams, author of many books and articles, was well known as a leader in international women's and children's movements.

Government Involvement in Social Services

The Great Depression provided the motivation and the basis for the majority of our current government-operated help-giving organizations. The massive failure of the economic system provided a broad-based understanding of poverty. The crushing demand for social services was beyond the resources of private charitable organizations, and existing state and local government agencies proved to be inadequate. Partly as a result of this inadequacy of government agencies to respond to the crisis, the Social Security Act of 1935 came into existence. This act clearly indicated the direct involvement of the federal government in the welfare of its citizens. The federal government's direct intervention in the personal and social problems of people continued throughout the Roosevelt administration and was heightened by population mobility, which rose dramatically prior to World War II. Prior to 1930, the private sector, motivated by a sense of charity, provided a variety of services to the needy. Services provided by privately funded charities were generally less expensive. They ranged from personal counseling and child welfare to recreational services. More expensive services, which were no longer made available through the extended family, became the responsibility of the federal and state governments—especially custodial programs. Some interest was evidenced by the private sector, but there were no consistent policies for coordinating publicly and privately funded programs; there was no coordination in terms of clientele to be served, referral processes, funding priorities, or criteria for evaluation.

The veterans who returned home after World War II created increased demands for a wide variety of services. These demands produced a major commitment of the federal government through the Veterans Administration. The addition of social and health services as a part of labor union contracts encouraged the federal government to become even more involved in the delivery of services. In addition, there was further acceleration in social mobility following World War II and a rapid change in the structure of family life and communities. New demands for services triggered a dramatic growth in professional training programs.

Barnes and Teeters

Prior to 1950, formally organized and specialized service programs were developed to replace the informal family-based and informal helping organizations of an earlier period. However, little progress had been made in the areas of criminal justice and corrections. In *New Horizons in Criminology*, Barnes and Teeters (1943) pointed out that imprisonment and other punishments for criminal behavior were mainly by courts. They urged their readers to recognize that the average criminal is a human who has been impelled by personal handicaps and unfortunate surroundings to commit a crime. According to Barnes and Teeters, conviction and imprisonment are frequently the result of helplessness and injustice. They claimed that a civilized philosophy of crime and criminals should stress the elimination of the causes of crime and the isolation of diseased and defective individuals who are prone to criminal behavior. Furthermore, Barnes and Teeters claimed that a rational treatment of crime and criminals demands a complete overhauling of our criminal law. Obsolete and trivial offenses should be eliminated, and serious offenses against public order and social well-being should be brought within the reach of justice. They did not overlook the importance of the apprehension system:

> Since we cannot handle criminals by even the most enlightened methods unless we have them in hand, we must improve our present methods of apprehending suspects and of convicting the guilty. . . . The jury system must be supplanted by a professional board of experts, trained in all the sciences essential to ascertaining guilt and guided solely by impartial interest in the facts available [Barnes & Teeters, 1943, p. 14].

Those of you who are interested in the study of criminal justice should review the work of Barnes and Teeters. More than 30 years ago, these two authors described an "ideal" treatment for criminals. They maintained that judges cannot have all the information required to rule on the type of treatment or the period of time for which criminals should be imprisoned. These facts can be determined only after careful investigation of the convicts and their behavior while they are in an institution. Barnes and Teeters pleaded for elaborate case histories to give some preliminary notion of how to design a rehabilitation program. They urged their readers to be far more courageous in extending probation to adult convicts, and they emphasized the importance of professionally trained probation officers. They suggested that a detailed examination of inmates would probably reveal that a considerable number of convicts cannot be reformed. They felt that these convicts should be shifted to institutions for the insane, degenerates, and incurables, whereas other convicts should be placed in humanely administered penal institutions that could be made self-supporting. Barnes and Teeters felt that, between these two extremes of those who should be handled through probation and those who should be permanently segregated as nonreformable, there would be a considerable group of convicts who would respond to rehabilitative treatment.

Barnes and Teeters emphasized the importance of unrestrained prison industries in the development of interest in reformatory discipline and economics; these industries should focus on the development of saleable skills. They felt that no convict should be released until suitable employment has been found. Such release to employment should be coupled very closely with a sound parole system. They concluded that their ideas won't be approached until the punitive philosophy of conventional prisons is abolished. Anything short of such abolishment would be no more than a superficial and contradictory attempt to humanize what are essentially savage institutions and practices.

Civil Rights and Equal Opportunity through Education

In the late 1950s, the federal government's involvement in human-service delivery was stimulated by the Civil Rights Movement and the conviction that local services for all citizens should be assured by national control and direction. During the 1960s, the federal administration and the Congress responded to almost every emergent problem of our riot-torn and turbulent society with new programs, each of which required separate funds and administrative staffs. Moreover, during the 1960s, the community-mental-health movement began to be accepted.

In the early 1960s, we developed long series of highly specialized problems in narrowly defined categories of clients. It is only within the past few years that we have discovered some of the negative aspects of this extreme specialization. The "categorical approach," which is commonly used to describe many piecemeal strategies of the planning and delivery of human services, is now severely criticized. For example, in the late 1950s and early 1960s, the emerging technologies of psychological assessment allowed us to place the children in our schools in very discrete categories. Universities responded with very specialized training programs. Affluent school districts responded by providing a wide array of specialized learning environments and specially trained teachers. Public Law 94-142, passed by Congress in 1975, deemphasizes these categories and, in fact, demands that the schools return to educating children in environments that are as normal as possible.

As long as there was a demand for unskilled workers who had a minimum education, teachers were free to weed out students who were unable to learn and focus their attention on the education and specialization of students who exhibited skill. Technology has reduced dramatically the need for unskilled workers. However, much thought and effort were directed to the final products of the educational system—those who successfully graduated—and, as a result, the system's assumptions and methods were rarely questioned. Social changes and technological advances have affected the entire fabric of our society, including the educational system. Our rapidly developing, complex urban and industrial society requires people who are highly literate and responsive to rapid changes in every area of life and work. In order to be successful, individuals must be able to learn and relearn complex ideas and skills; those who do not succeed are treated as deviants in need of resocialization.

Individuals' beliefs are sometimes more important than their actions. The United States has been shaped by a widely shared belief in the idea of equality. The early settlers in the Northeast favored individual and congregational responsibility over the authority of priesthood. Individual landholding was made possible by vast resources. Property meant status; large numbers of individuals held property and, therefore, equal status. Based on the assumption that "all men are created equal," the Union was founded on ideas of political democracy that were socially reinforced by the expanding frontier. Moreover, the belief that one individual is as good as another and that one person's opinion and vote have equal status with another's is firmly rooted in the U.S. consciousness. The economic and social counterparts of that belief have come to be accepted, but few of these high-sounding claims have been translated into action.

Dramatic changes in the 20th century have created new polarities and pressures in the U.S. The disgruntled or unemployed can no longer head for the woods, find a new home, and depend on the land for existence. The ill and incapable require care. The thief is no longer beaten and kicked. The therapy of turning the soil to settle the sickness of the soul has given way to clever men who test our laws, norms, and mores. We have moved into an urbanized and technological world.

Our society and our government have responded to "unsuccessfully socialized" individuals with a variety of treatments. The goal is to bring these individuals back into the mainstream. The general term describing this process is *resocialization.* We attempt to provide skill-training programs for the unemployed, educational programs for underachievers, rehabilitation for convicted law violators, physical health for medical patients, comfort and long life for the aged, and therapy for child abusers. The core of all such treatment modes is education.

Education as the Answer

Although Horace Mann's name stands in the forefront of early public education, other individuals made significant contributions. As early as the 1860s, the connection was made between the need for educational development and the problem of social order, morality, and crime in a society that was increasingly characterized by factories and cities. This connection was pointed out by Henry Barnard (1865). He addressed the issue of school attendance, which he characterized as the most immediate and perplexing issue faced by promoters of public education throughout the country. As we will see, this issue remains unresolved today. Throughout its history, the United States has turned to educational reform in the hope that it would improve the quality of life in the cities. Nearly 100 years after the publication of Barnard's article, Conant (1961) authored *Slums and Suburbs;* the publication of this book was followed by President Johnson's War on Poverty, which resulted in the passage of the Elementary and Secondary Education Act of 1965.

Three Major Areas of Concern in Educational Reform

Three major areas of concern in educational reform are: early childhood education, juvenile delinquency, and compulsory school attendance. In the past, educational reformists focused their attention on these areas, and they continue to do so today. Let's look briefly at each of these areas of concern.

Early Childhood Education. The beginning of early childhood education was marked by two lines of thought regarding its basic purpose. The first line of thought attempted to link the conditions of urban life to the disintegration of the family and the neglect of the urban child. The second, which continues today, deals with early development of the skills needed to cope in society through the development of morality. These two concerns were fused very easily. Early in U.S. history, education, like many other institutions, was based on an English model. The concept of infant education, imported from England, enjoyed a brief and intense popularity in the United States during the 1820s.

Movements aimed at improving urban life and education, then and now, stress the early schooling of the city child. In the 1850s, primary schools were staffed by female teachers, who acted as surrogate mothers. This was quickly followed by the introduction of the kindergarten on a wide scale. One of the hallmarks of educational reform in the 1960s was Operation Headstart.

Juvenile Delinquency. The second major area of concern in educational reform can be traced from the opening of the first state reformatory at Westborough, Massachusetts in 1848. Early reform schools were explicitly regarded as integral parts of public school systems, and they reflected the 19th century belief that education and crime were related. This belief was supported in 1881 by the Wickersham Report (Wickersham, 1881). Reform schools were expanded, and they became common; however, despite this expansion, delinquency did not disappear. Its causes, treatment, and prevention remain matters of controversy today. As late as 1967, a balanced assessment of the research of delinquency was presented in *The Challenge of Crime in a Free Society* (1967), a report submitted by a presidential committee on law enforcement in the administration of justice. This report establishes a connection between the failures of our schools and the spread of crime among youths.

Compulsory School Attendance. In 1851, Massachusetts passed the first compulsory-education law. The debate over the desirability of compulsory education continued in some areas of the country well into the 20th century. Compulsory attendance, like the idea of public education, was linked to the alleviation of the problem of crime in urban society. In 1961 the secretary of labor suggested that education be made mandatory to age 18 in order to serve the national interest (Wirtz, 1964). Both Wirtz and Conant (1961) argued from familiar traditional positions. Their arguments regarding compulsory education were similar to those expressed by Henry Barnard 100 years earlier.

Why has public education failed to bring about improvement in the life of the city and its people? Is that a reasonable goal? These questions deserve thoughtful discussion.

What Are the Functions of a School?

Should the interest of the individual student take precedence over the interests of the larger society? Is the inculcation of socially accepted attitudes more important than the improvement of the intellect? In other words, do schools exist primarily to train the mind or to form character? These questions were raised as early as 1856 (*The Massachusetts Teacher*, 1856). To what extent should schools be practical? Should general and enduring values guide the development of curriculum, or should instruction be focused on the development of skills and competencies that students will need in the pursuit of a job or in their general lives? In the late 19th century and early 20th century, this debate over the functions of schools continued. Charges that schools were trying to do too much were added to the debate; some people felt that traditional, intellectual training was being diluted. In 1900, many people argued that schools were assuming responsibilities that belonged to the family, the church, and the community (*The Massachusetts Teacher*, 1850). Echoes of these arguments are heard today. By what process should children be taught? Arguments over pedagogy versus content remain unsettled.

Universal public education originated from a variety of impulses and motives. As the political philosophy underlying the Revolutionary War was translated into voting practices, all people, including the poor, needed an education. The beginning of industrial technology led to an increased demand for skilled workers. Though their motives appeared to be appropriate, those in control were clearly the "establishment." The power that drove the educational process was largely conservative and racist. These historical hallmarks characterize public education today, especially in urban public schools.

The approaches to educating Black children in the North were simply a reflection of the early attitudes developed in the

1850s toward poor White children of immigrant families. Educators developed a set of strategies to deal with these children and a set of patronizing assumptions that advocated the use of schools as agents of "Americanization." The poor and the immigrants, White and Black alike, were treated as essentially different and inferior (*The Massachusetts Teacher*, 1851). In the course of a century, the object of overt early racism shifted from poor Whites to Blacks.

On the assumption that some people are inferior, educators have frequently shifted the blame for educational failure from the inadequate performance of the schools to the inherited limitations of their students (*The Unitarian Review*, 1876). The modern phrase that reflects this position is "cultural deprivation." Late in the 18th century, children of poor families exhibited academic problems in the segregated public schools of Northern cities. The first Black school was opened in 1798 and existed for almost 50 years. This author attended a 15-room elementary school in eastern Pennsylvania in the early 1940s that contained one room for Black children, regardless of their grade level. Segregation in U.S. schools was widespread, despite efforts begun as early as 1849 by a group of Blacks who petitioned the Boston School Committee to abolish segregation in the schools. The committee rejected their petition (Boston School Committee, 1849). Throughout the past 125 years, the belief that the poor are inferior has remained strong, although the basis of that belief has shifted from a moral philosophy to a social science theory, which is more appropriate to our age.

The Cult of Efficiency

Many White Americans traced their ancestry from the underprivileged of Europe. They had little or no tradition of learning or scholarship. Their main interest was material wealth. Their idols were Carnegie, Rockefeller, and Vanderbilt. In both their speaking and writing, these successful industrialists did not credit book learning for their success; they claimed that energy, initiative, hard work, and common sense made them successful. The influence of these well-known and successful industrialists became evident with the increasing emphasis on industrial education in public schools.

Effective and efficient workers were needed for industry. Between 1865 and 1900, immigrants came to this country at a rate of more than 1 million per year. They lived in the Eastern cities, where their children entered school. Predominantly from poor socioeconomic groups, these non-English speaking children from semiliterate families created educational problems that were unparalleled in history. These problems were highlighted in 1909 by the publication of Leonard Ayres' *Laggards in Our Schools* (cited in Callahan, 1962). Not only did Ayres report the percentages of "retarded" children attending public schools, which ranged from 7% to 75% depending on the school, but he also characterized the school as a factory to which the principles of industry and business could be applied in a systematic way.

In 1910, the United States was dazzled by the principle of "scientific management." Fredrick W. Taylor convinced the Interstate Commerce Commission that the railroads did not need to increase their freight rates in order to compensate for an earlier wage hike given to the workers. He suggested that railroad management be revised. The Taylor System was quickly translated for application to the armed services, the legal profession, the home, the family, and even the church. In 1914, *Scientific Management in Education* was published in Chicago by J. M. Rice, physician and educator. Soon thereafter, the World Book Company produced a series of management handbooks based on Taylor's model of efficient management.

The new age of efficiency had a dramatic impact on public schools. The groundwork had been laid for general suspicion of all public institutions. The jails had failed, the insane remained ill, and the public schools had not cured delinquency. It was about this time that Taylor introduced his system with his convincing testimony before the Interstate Commerce Commission. The status and prestige of a small group of successful businessmen had influenced the election of business-oriented people to the management of public schools and other public institutions. Moreover, the "profession" of school administration had been introduced; however, the profession had no tradition. It was influenced by Taylor's principles. Leading school administrators and their trainers saw schools as enterprises from which students received their diplomas on schedule. John Dewey (1929, p. 15) saw the problem quite clearly. He warned educators that it was very easy for science "to be regarded as a guarantee that goes with the sale of goods rather than as a light to the eyes and a lamp to the feet."

It would please me to report that change had occurred in the development of educational administration; unfortunately, such is not the case. Some attempts have been made, and some progress has occurred. There was a partial disenchantment with business leadership as a result of the Great Depression; however, most schools today operate on Taylor's model.

Bureaucratic Administration

The final issue to be discussed in our brief treatment of the history of public education is bureaucratic administration. During the 1850s, there was little coordination among public schools. Wide variety existed within and between communities. The introduction of a centralized high school was intended to "standardize" the local educational arrangement basic to the needed educational reform at the time. There was opposition, of course, especially from those who operated private schools. This debate, and the issues it raised, were published in the *Massachusetts Teacher*. The journal's editor was very supportive of public education. A contrasting view of public education was presented by the forces who owned and controlled so-called free academies. The threat of the emergent public high schools elicited a campaign by the owners of private academies, who made claims about the superior virtue of a private education. One hundred twenty years later, the theme of the private academies was echoed by Berthoff who wrote "the public school itself was a true 'parochial' school. Indeed, as keeper and official inculcator of the amalgam of economic and 'idealistic' values later to be identified as the American Way of Life, the public school was the closest approximation to an American established church" (Berthoff, 1971, p. 440).

The administrative disarray, especially of urban schools, was characterized by an elected school board charged with the management of the grammar and high school. A series of separate boards administered the many small primary schools scattered throughout an urban area. Typically, these schools did not communicate. Little or no coordination existed between the several levels of education in large urban areas. Reformers desired not only centralization but also professional superintendents. These two issues were widely publicized through the publication of *The School and the School Master* (Potter & Emerson, 1842).

By 1870, urban education in the U.S. had become carefully differentiated, rule bound, and run by specialists. The system was very hierarchical. The advocates of high school education had successfully introduced careful age-rating and skill-rating procedures into the school system. Professional administrators were in full command.

Following quickly on the heels of these developments was a shift in the size and composition of school boards. Prior to 1900, most urban school boards were very large, and they were influenced, to an extent, by politics. In the spirit of the city-government-reform movement of the early 1900s, school board membership shifted from a wide diversity of backgrounds toward businessmen, and the size of the boards was reduced. For instance, in Boston school board membership dropped from 24 to 5 members. As we will see later, these changes in composition were to have far-reaching impact on public schools.

Mental Health

Largely because it is a relatively young concept, the history of the mental-health movement has been overshadowed in this chapter by criminal justice, social work, and education. In England, as well as in the colonial United States, the insane were one of a number of subcategories of the poor. The question "What caused them to be poor?" was not considered seriously. If their families were unable to provide care, the insane were eligible to be taken care of by the church.

The larger communities in the colonies built the first insane asylums—sometimes a single room on public property. Extreme cases that became too disruptive to the family were housed in these rooms at public expense. These single-room facilities were closed with the advent of the almshouse. The insane were housed with widows, orphans, and the physically handicapped. The use of the poorhouses to shelter the insane was followed by the use of jails to house "lunatics." This practice continued into the 1830s, and even later in some communities.

The Worcester (Massachusetts) State Lunatic Hospital, which was opened in 1833, was the first mental hospital in the United States. The major stimulus for the construction of the hospital was the widely publicized poor housing conditions of the insane in jails. Additional stimulus to the mental-hospital movement was provided by reports from Europe that indicated that almost one-half of one group of mental patients had recovered when placed in a hospital, and that early intervention resulted in a 90% recovery rate. These reports also stimulated the development of a classification system for the insane that was instituted in the new Worcester State Lunatic Hospital.

State hospitals for the insane became commonplace in every state within 100 years. Dairy herds and other agriculturally related activities were associated with the mental hospitals, because most of these institutions were located in rural areas. A few private mental hospitals were supported by individuals who could afford private care. The state mental hospital, as an institution, flourished during a 100-year period. Not until the late 1950s and early 1960s was the institutional model of treatment seriously challenged. The challenge came through the community mental-health movement. One of the immediate outcomes of this movement was a shift to a reduction in the size of hospitalized patient populations.

The transfer of mental patients from hospitals to nursing homes and other shelter-care institutions was supported by both federal and state legislation during the 1960s. Categorical federal legislation not only supported deinstitutionalization but also founded community mental-health activities aimed at secondary prevention on a local level. Primary prevention, in the form of outreach programs, street therapy, and family treatment, has, in a sense, brought us full circle to the early colonial model of treatment—the family and the immediate environment have again become the preferred locus of treatment. This rediscovery is enhanced by a growing body of professional knowledge, a cadre of well-trained workers, and governmental support.

Government Service and Control

Why have governments become involved in health, education, and social welfare? The answer appears to lie in three interrelated motives: (1) to avoid social unrest, (2) to acquire political power, and (3) to provide services as a part of the political process.

The desire to avoid social unrest motivated the passage of the Poor Laws of England. Roving bands of beggars often turned to robbery or pillage; therefore, some people argued that relief for the poor (supposedly designed for humanitarian reasons) was actually conceived as a measure that would reduce the potential danger of desperate action by this part of the population. Similarly, the Civilian Conservation Corps legislation enacted during the Great Depression was not only a response to the employment and welfare needs of the time; it also was a response to the "bonus marchers," who, in 1932, were dispersed by the force of federal and state troops and housed in abandoned army camps.

As a result of the Great Depression, large numbers of politicians began to attract followings by their proposals to overcome the effects of the then current economic situation. One of the most influential politicians was Francis Townsend, who devised a plan to relieve the poverty of the aged and contribute to the economic recovery of the country. The plan was quite simple. Every person over the age of 60 was to receive $200 a month, provided that the money was spent within 30 days. The plan was to be financed by a sales tax. The poor would have money to spend, and they would have to spend it. The demand for consumer goods would go up and provide jobs. For all of this, a sales tax would be a small price to pay. The Townsend plan gained an estimated 10 million supporters and 12,000 organized clubs by the end of 1934 (Moynihan, 1969).

It is clear that the Social Security Act represented, at least in part, a desire to reduce the political power of the Townsend movement, which had become strong enough to begin endorsing political candidates and, in some cases, even nominating its own candidates. There have been other instances in which the political power (or the potential political power) of a group led to the passage of social-welfare programs. One example of this is the GI Bill of Rights. No other status group was as well rewarded as the veterans of World War II. Although the GI Bill of Rights is not explicitly a social-welfare program, it represents one of the most successful instances of social welfare without socialism.

Some social services are side effects of the political process. For instance, when war or defense installations are built, an array of schools, clinics, and recreational facilities are required. During World War II, many defense plants in the United States were staffed by women who had dependent children. The government was in the child-care business. Whenever a full-employment program is passed, it leads to the need for training schools, apprenticeship programs, and child-care facilities.

By examining some of the possible reasons and arguments for government involvement in helping, you may be able to gain some insights into the reason for your career decision. One point of view, represented by the socialist schools, is that the capitalist system of private enterprise and a free market economy is unjust and inefficient and should be replaced by government planning and direction. In such a case, this point of view contends, people's needs would be met, and some needs would cease to exist, because poverty would not exist. For example, the Soviet Union provides a universal children's allowance and requires no contribution by employees to maintain social-insurance programs; such programs are financed by employer and government contributions.

Another viewpoint maintains that social problems can be remedied by government intervention. The conservative position holds that the deficiencies in our current social-economic policies will be corrected in the normal course of events. It appears that the current philosophy in the United States is represented in the following statement: "Yes, there are problems, but these problems are not created by any basic defect in our governmental or economic systems. All we need is government intervention to reduce some of the natural problems."

The United States has been reluctant to accept the label of "a welfare state." Herbert Hoover described a welfare state as a disguise for a totalitarian state, and claimed that, if we went much further, we would be on the last mile to collectivism (Titmuss, 1967). A contemporary translation of this position has deep historical roots. It is widely accepted that individuals who are supported by the welfare state lose their sense of responsibility and the ability to make their own decisions. It is feared that such people will no longer be concerned with the future and, therefore, will not be motivated to work, to save, or to plan ahead—they will continue to be a drain on the economy. On the other hand, even the strongest advocates of a welfare state agree that it has failed to eliminate socially defined poverty. In the United States, the principles of the welfare state have not been incorporated into basic laws. The courts have not found a right to social welfare in the U.S. Constitution.

The acceptance of a middle position between what I have characterized as socialistic and conservative viewpoints is reflected in the policies and behaviors of the federal government. The legislative and appropriating processes of the federal government require that social-welfare and mental-health programs be designed in specific legislation to alleviate specific social problems. Even after Congress has authorized the funds to implement specific legislation, it has been the prerogative of recent presidents to impound or withhold funds, usually in the name of a balanced budget. The effects of such governmental behavior create instability and uncertainty at the local level. Last-minute funding results in waste and poor implementation; long-range local and state planning is made impossible, and opportunistic programming and rapid shifting of professional staff result. The basic problem is that the United States has no formal planning machinery for long-term strategies in health, welfare, education, mental health, and criminal justice.

Summary

The purpose of this chapter has been to help you locate yourself in time. The organization for which you work (or will work) has a long history. The specific agency may be new, but its roots go deep into the social and cultural past. The established employees will have felt the impact of this past. They may have reacted to the history with cynicism and hopelessness. Conditions have improved, and you can be a part of that improvement.

A brief look at history may clarify some of your reasons for choosing a career in human service. At a minimum, it will provide a different perspective. A general idea of how our present bureaucratic help giving has grown from its historical roots will be an aid to you in maintaining a balance between your personal and professional responsibilities. Using this brief history in a different way, you can gain a new perspective on your relationships with clients, administrators, legislators, regulators, and program evaluators.

It is commonly believed that history has real predictive value—that, by understanding what has happened, we can anticipate the future. Such a belief doesn't stand the test when you look closely. Past actions did produce consequences that can be studied. It is tempting to conclude that, if we take the same action now, the same consequences will occur; however, the context of the present differs radically from that of the past. Historical analogies can be useful, but they are subtle, delicate, and complex. Careless use of such analogies can sometimes be worse than total historical ignorance. We can't look to history for prediction and hope, but we can use it to gain perspective. History locates us in time. By locating ourselves and our jobs, we can better understand the context in which we live and work. History takes us back to the origins of our present problems. If you understand these origins, you will be more likely to be effective in your efforts to serve clients and make meaningful change without burning out.

Most likely, you won't be a Horace Mann, Dorothea Dix, or John Dewey, but look closer to home. Your own unit, your own class load, your own floor, or your own department may provide the best place for you to begin. Tackle something that looks small enough to handle. Even if the first try doesn't succeed, study and record what went wrong and how you'll do it differently next time.

Discussion Questions

1. Why have you chosen to be a help giver? What other careers have you considered?
2. How did you move from those earlier decisions to your present one?
3. What are the greatest changes that need to be made in the service area you have selected? Do you intend to attempt to make any changes in your service area? If so, which ones and how do you plan to go about it?

4. Disregarding constitutional issues, do you believe that the "jury of peers" system should be replaced by "a panel of experts" in criminal trials?
5. Why have public schools been and continue to be blamed for most of society's ills?
6. Do you think that a public school is really a government-run parochial school?
7. Is the U.S. government involved in social welfare for humanitarian reasons?

References

Barnard, H. The sixth annual report of the superintendent of common schools to the general assembly of Connecticut for 1865. *American Journal of Education*, 1865, *5*, 293–310.

Barnes, H. E., & Teeters, N. K. *New horizons in criminology: The American crime problem.* New York: Prentice-Hall, 1943.

Berthoff, R. T. *An unsettled people: Social order and disorder in American history.* New York: Harper & Row, 1971.

Boston School Committee. Report of a special committee of the grammar school board, presented August 29, 1849, on the petition of sundry colored persons praying for the abolition of the Smith School, Boston, 1849.

Brennecke, J. H., & Amick, R. G. *The struggle for significance.* Beverly Hills: Glencoe Press, 1975.

Callahan, R. E. *Education and the cult of efficiency.* Chicago: University of Chicago Press, 1962.

The challenge of crime in a free society. Report by the President's committee on law enforcement in the administration of justice, 1967, *3*, 56–71.

Conant, J. B. *Slums and suburbs.* New York: McGraw-Hill, 1961.

Dewey, J. *The sources of a science education.* New York: Harper & Row, 1929.

Federico, R. C. *The social welfare institution: An introduction* (2nd ed.). Lexington, Mass.: D. C. Heath & Co., 1976.

Gilbert, N., & Specht, H. *The emergence of social welfare and social work.* Itasca, Ill.: F. E. Peacock Publishers, Inc., 1976.

Kamerman, S. B., & Kahn, A. J. *Social services in the United States: Policies and programs.* Philadelphia: Temple University Press, 1976.

Lubobe, R. *The professional altruist: The emergence of social work as a career 1880–1930.* Forge Village, New York: Atheneum, 1969.

Massachusetts Teacher, Editorial, February 1850, *3*, 49.

Massachusetts Teacher, Immigration. *4*, 1851, 289–291.

Massachusetts Teacher, Editorial, September 1856, *9*, 398–403.

Messerli, J. *Horace Mann: A biography.* New York: Alfred A. Knopf, 1972.

Moynihan, D. P. *The politics of a guaranteed income: The Nixon administration and the family assistance plan.* New York: Free Press, 1969.

Peabody, A. The relation of the public schools to the civil government. *The Unitarian Review*, July 1876, *6*, 24–39. (Originally taken from an address before the Massachusetts Convention of Teachers given in Boston, January 5, 1876.)

Potter, P., & Emerson, G. B. *The school and the school master: A manual for the use of teachers, employers, trustees, and inspectors, etc., of the mon schools.* New York: Harper & Brothers, 1842.

Rothman, D. J. *The discovery of the asylum: Social order and disorder in the New Republic.* Boston-Toronto: Little, Brown, 1971.

Titmuss, R. M. In C. I. Schottland (Ed.), *The welfare state: Images and realities.* New York: Harper & Row, 1967.

Walsh, A. H. *The urban challenge to government.* New York: Praeger, 1969.

Wickersham, J. P. Education and crime. *The Journals and Proceedings and Address of the National Education Association of the United States Session of the Year 1881* (2nd day proceedings), 1881, 45-55.

Wirtz, W. W. *Remarks of the Honorable W. Willard Wirtz.* Presented in a symposium on employment, sponsored by the American Bankers Association, Washington, D.C., 1964.

3 The People

The people your organization helps—clients, students, inmates, or wards—are the reason for your job. They have their own view of you, their own view of all the other people who are employed by your organization, and their own view of one another. Clients have a lot of things in common with you, and with one another, because you're all human. People need air, water, food, physical security, psychological security, acceptance, love, opportunity for growth, and the need to be needed by another human being. Jourard (1964), Maslow (1962), May (1950), and O'Banion and O'Connell (1970) are a few of the well known psychologists who have written like poets about human needs. Each of them has a special set of words to tell us how we feel; however, we don't need psychologists to tell us about loneliness or what it feels like to be hurt by a partner. Toffler (1970) documents this fact in *Future Shock*. Keesing (1974) has shown that the trend toward "transient" relationships is illustrated in today's lyrics. Young people are bombarded by music that reflects the need to belong, even if the belonging is temporary.

Clients

The need to be important—to count—is felt by all of us, including the clients and staff members with whom you work. If you look carefully at each person as an individual, you will see behavior that indicates this need. The need to be recognized as a human being is sometimes so strong in people who have been consistently ignored that it comes out in bizarre ways. Mental patients often demonstrate this need dramatically. A psychiatric worker describes the following incidents:

> Half the problems arise out of sheer desperation. They need attention so bad sometimes, they want somebody to talk to so bad that they walk up and down, up and down, up and down. The morning shift ought to ask, "What's wrong, Harold?" Nobody asks. Harold walks by three or four times and finally he gets angry. He knocks the ashtray over. Then everybody comes jumping around to catch him and give him a shot. Harold's happy. He's smiling. He's got all the attention. Another patient would break windows . . . and cut herself up just to get attention. She'd be really happy with the doctor patching her up. Then she'd wander. Sometimes they'd give her a shot, but she wouldn't lie down, or she'd get out of bed and punch through another window. So they'd tell me to sit in her window, and they'd tie her down. Later, when she was untied, this girl starts stripping, and she's really beautiful. She'd sit and she'd masturbate in front of me.

Maybe you've never experienced anything like this, but you can remember the kid at school who was the expert brinkman—the one who could push the rules to the fine line. The books falling on the floor by "accident," the loud cough, the loud laughter, all take place in front of an audience. These things are all disguised in order to keep the culprit out of real trouble. The profanity is always spoken in a low voice—but it's loud enough for the other students to hear. Willower (Licata & Willower, 1975) has enjoyed studying what he calls "student brinkmanship." He found that students do these things in school not only to demonstrate their skill but also to get attention from other people.

Your clients are people in the system who are trying to meet their needs. Their behavior may demand much of your attention; you may forget that they are a lot like you. This is especially true of new staff members, because, except in unusual circumstances, new employees are assigned to the toughest clients, the slowest classes, the least desirable shift, the hardest case load, the most boring work station, and the least convenient schedule. A beginning teacher puts it this way:

> I had five different classes, each with a different preparation.

All but one of these classes was in the lowest track. Oh, the chairman—well, she teaches an honors English and two accelerated English classes.

In many general hospitals, beginning nurses work the evening shift. One nurse explained this phenomenon:

> It's the shift that has the least help. You have as much to do as you do on days, but you have less people and it's hard to get ahold of doctors, partly because you know they are not coming in. Also, you hesitate to call them, because, being on evenings, you don't really get to know the doctors who usually make their rounds in the morning.

A new prison guard thought he would select the shift he wanted:

> I told him [the captain] that I didn't care to go on the night shift—that I would prefer to stay on the day shift. He told me that it was up to me: either I went on the night shift or I went out the door, so the choice was not that large. I was on the night shift for about a year, and I worked almost all assignments on the night shift. I worked cell houses, front and back barracks, the towers, the yard watch, the guard hall, and the arsenal.

You want to help the clients. You may seek help from more experienced staff members. If you are frustrated in your attempts to obtain help in one-to-one talks with coworkers, you might decide to try to get help for your clients in a more formal situation, like a staff meeting:

> In the teacher meetings that we would have, I would mention things that I would like to do with my class. Once, I asked about team teaching. Another teacher and I tried this, and right away we were told it was out. I tried to talk about how I felt about my kids, the things they did and how I tried to deal with them. I got the feeling that people were talking behind my back and, at times, saying things like "Follow the rules and don't cause any trouble or try to change anything, because we don't want to have to do it."

An institutional nurse, in discussing the fact that some of the students needed eyeglasses, tried to get help through her supervisor. Later, she brought up the issue at a staff meeting and received this answer:

"We don't do things like that here. Our budget isn't set up for that." And when I'd ask "Well, who is *we?*" nobody could tell me who *we* was. So, between "We've never done it that way" and "We've always done it this way," I hit one brick wall after another.

The clients you confront will behave in ways that may seem very confusing. They will try to find out as quickly as possible what kind of a person you are and how far you're going to go in meeting their needs.

Attempts to help clients in ways that are outside established rules can take a variety of forms. For instance, in the typical state agency, budget lines for materials and supplies for direct use by clients are extremely limited.

> Sometimes we have money-making projects like cake sales. Presently, we have a monthly dinner, the proceeds of which go to the patients' fund. We buy such things as a hair dryer for the women on the ward and cigarettes and soda for those who don't have any money. A simple thing like a comb is very often the hardest thing to come across. Many packs of cigarettes, soda, coffee, and combs are bought for patients by employees on the ward. Each employee decides just how generous to be and how often to be "taken." The results of this are that some of the patients have begun to expect such presents in the normal course of events. When some of us don't feel we have the personal funds to do these kind of things, the patients respond to us like we really didn't care about them. Even though we meant to do good, I think this kind of activity has interfered with our treatment program.

When clients are in a group, they seek to gain the acceptance and status among their peers. Prison inmates test a new correctional officer. Ambulatory hospital patients try to see how many doors they can get you to unlock with your new set of keys. Detention-home residents want to find out how many extra telephone calls you will allow them to place. Students, prison inmates, patients, and residents all need to know how flexible you are willing to be on the institutional time schedule. Do you start class on time, turn out the lights when you're supposed to, do bed check thoroughly and on time, stay to see they have taken their medicine, and other routine institutional matters? They need to know what, if any, changes you plan to try to make in either the written or the unwritten rules.

The clients have had experience with a number of other authority figures, and they have learned how to live with them.

In this sense, they have an advantage, especially if this is the first time you have been in a position of authority. They are experienced, and you are not. If you choose to make it a battle, the odds are with them, not only because they are more experienced but also because they outnumber you. Usually, institutional staff members are outnumbered by clients. Jacobs, a criminologist, and Retsky, a former prison guard turned counselor, describe the ways in which inmates can jeopardize a guard's job, especially by messing up the "count" (the counting process that takes place several times a day) (Jacobs & Retsky, 1975). On the other hand, if you see the situation as an opportunity for you to learn and for the clients to help you learn, the chances of your relationship becoming a battle are reduced. The danger in this attitude is that the clients may seduce you into becoming so concerned about their personal welfare that you lose your effectiveness in your job. Jacobs (1974) discusses the consequences when a new correctional officer takes on the role of a counselor. In the belief that he is helping the rehabilitation process, the new guard may take the correctional process into his own hands by allowing the inmates more privileges than the rules allow. According to Jacobs, the consequences of this arrangement are usually negative.

In most correctional institutions, the security officers use a system of written reports, or "tickets," to describe inmate misbehavior. These tickets may lead to a form of punishment, such as the revocation of a previously earned privilege. An inmate told a new guard that he was going to kill him. The guard chose not to write a ticket.

> Instead of that, I tried to calm him down. I tried to talk to him for most of the rest of my shift. He didn't want to talk, so, just before I left, I wrote up a ticket and turned it in. The next morning, as soon as I got to work, the inmate called me to his cell and apologized. We had a good discussion. He gave me a lot of commitments. I told him I would drop the ticket and simply write up an incident report, which would go into his jacket [file] but wouldn't be considered a disciplinary violation. I went to the captain's office to have him drop the ticket so I could write an incident report. The captain told me he didn't have the power to let me take the ticket back—I would have to talk to the unit commander. The unit commander refused to let me dismiss the ticket and said that all violations are punished. I then called the warden in charge of security, and he said the ticket would be handled and processed. It was out of my hands. The inmate went to the hole for 15 days.

I was in a bad light with the captain, the unit commander, and the warden. When the inmate came out, he said he held no hard feelings, but he seemed apathetic about the whole deal.

This incident was followed by another poor judgment on my part. Two men had been killed in the cell house on _____. Very soon thereafter, five security officers were taken hostage in the cell unit for about three hours but released unharmed. The warden put the whole institution in dead lock [all inmates locked in their cells 24 hours a day]. Our unit had not been involved in either of these incidents, and I thought it was unjust. Our unit shouldn't be treated like all of the rest. The warden and the unit commander told me they felt the same way and told me that, if the rest of the guards on our unit agreed, he would not put our men on dead lock. I put it to a vote. I was the only vote to let them out. This got me off to a bad start with the other guards but got me a lot of help from the inmates. One example was that a fairly new inmate tried to give me a hard time one day about trying to get into his cell, and the rest of the men told him to quit giving me a hard time.

As I look back now, my behavior in both of these incidents has been one of the major factors in my not being promoted. The chief guard and my lieutenant have blocked every promotion that I have tried to get in the last 3½ years.

Your Feelings about Clients

Do you dislike your clients because of the way they behave? Do you disapprove of your clients' behavior but still accept them as human beings? The people you're there to help need to know what kinds of things threaten you and what kinds of things you can deal with in a fair and objective manner. Maybe you don't know. It will help you to find out. A personal journal, in which you describe feelings about each day's (or night's) work, will give you some clues about your fears and your ability to deal with problems. I encourage you to experiment with the form of your journal. Here are a few suggestions that some people have found useful. Use a hardback book that opens flat for easier writing. Softback and loose-leaf books aren't very durable. A few key questions may help to guide you in your entries. You could write a factual description of each day's events—fill in the actors, the circumstances, and the outcomes. What did you do? What actions, if any, did you take? What alternatives did you have in the situation? You may find it helpful to use your journal for self-examination at the end of each week, month, or pay period.

Ask yourself questions such as "What kinds of clients attract me?" "Which clients repel me?" "What do I like most about what I am doing?" and "What do I like least about my job?"

The most important question to be answered in your daily journal is "How did I feel about what happened?" This is the hardest part for most of us. Feelings and emotions drive our behavior. *Sad, glad, happy, excited, disgusted, revolted, thrilled, anxious, pleased, warm,* and *angry* are words that should appear in your journal.

Dealing with Clients

As a human-service worker, you may find yourself in a situation in which the majority of those with whom you work really want help, but a very vocal minority constantly interferes with your efforts. In such a situation, how would you continue to help the majority and deal with the disruptive influence of those who appear to be saying "We don't want your help"? Maybe you will be forced to separate one group from the other until the majority is willing and able to help you control the "troublemakers." You may be good at your job, but you can't do all things for all people. The facts are that most inmates return to prison, many hospitalized mental patients are repeaters, delinquents can con you, some students don't want to learn, and clients aren't always truthful.

In the more typical case, in which the group seems to be saying (in unison) "We will tolerate you if you will tolerate us, but don't make changes or demands," the decision for you is much clearer. Some client groups, especially in institutions, will seem to say "If you don't bother us, we won't bother you." Smith (1968, p. 151) calls this *the contract* when he talks about classrooms. These kinds of contracts are never written down, but students and teachers know what's expected. Some clients have discovered that the way to get out is to be "rehabilitated." These clients may say "Tell us the rules of the game, and we will play." They learn exactly what you want and how you want it. They choose to play to get what they want—grades, welfare checks, or release. These clients have made an adjustment to an involuntary situation. They understand both the written and the unwritten rules, and they have learned, in their own way, how to live with them.

While your clients are trying to find out what makes you tick, you're trying to discover the most effective means of dealing with them. This tendency to "psych each other out" is especially strong during your first contacts; the tension produced by this process dissipates over time. Again, if you choose to make it a battle, the clients have a big advantage. As you try to psych out the clients, you try to learn about the people with whom you work, your immediate supervisor, and all the things you don't know about the organization that has hired you. When the clients push you during that first contact, stand your ground without being belligerent. If you choose to fight the clients, they will probably win. Perhaps you are thinking "No, I can beat them at this first skirmish, and I'm going to find out what makes them tick and be able to hide from them who I really am." However, your victory will be a temporary one only. The clients will learn quickly how you do battle, and they probably won't make the mistakes they made the first time, when you won. The kind of attitude that has helped new staff members is illustrated by an institutional nurse who said:

> All the employees here represent to that boy everybody that's helped to put him in this place. We personify the teacher he couldn't get along with, the cop that busted him, the probation officer that gave up on him, the judge that sentenced him, the state's attorney that prosecuted him, and even the transportation officer that brought him here. He has an extremely touchy sense of justice. Just the fact that another boy might have a bigger scoop of ice cream is an injustice. Once you're in tune with these feelings, I think it's easier to understand the kid. Administration divorces themselves from the everyday happenings in an institution. They send down a few memos here and there with a bunch of rules and regulations that you kind of have to work around. Our administrators don't even begin to understand this super fine sense of justice and injustice. I think actual helping starts after there is some mutual feeling, good and sometimes even bad, but honest feeling expressed—a little bit of trust starting to develop and the fact that the boy knows that you're going to be fair, that you're going to give him a fair shake.

Those of you who work on a one-to-one basis will go through a similar process with clients as they test you. For example, a mother receiving aid to dependent children support (ADC) may coach her children before you arrive. As a result, when you ask questions such as "Where is your father?" or "When does your mother get home from work?" the answers will be designed to maximize the amount of the next check. Most likely, the lies are not meant personally. You are seen as a representative of the system. The clients' survival depends on their ability to work with and use the system. The ADC mother may have dealt with other caseworkers before you; in that sense, she is more experienced than you are.

Similar examples are provided by mental-health workers who are hustled by clients who are dependent on drugs. The workers may discover that they have helped to secure a prescription from the supervising psychiatrist for a client's favorite drug. Even worse, the client may have used the new relationships with workers to "lift" a pad of prescription blanks. It hurts when you discover that you have been used. Your first response to being used may be to feel hurt and deceived. Unless you put them in a larger context, a series of such events may lead you to be cynical.

According to your personal set of values and beliefs, deception may be wrong. Perhaps you don't hurt people who are trying to help you. The client's values may differ from your own. For instance, the client may believe that deception is a profitable skill to be learned and practiced. Furthermore, people who represent the "system" are there to be used. Such values may not be to your liking.

The client's behavior reflects his or her values. One of your tasks may be to "help the client" change such values. Altering values and belief systems is usually a long-term process. Are you patient enough to absorb the feeling of being used in order to demonstrate a different value system?

Staff Members

Many established employees at all staff levels come across as cruel, indifferent, and incompetent. These employees may have been "burned out" by a series of events. At one time, they may have been a lot like you are now. Their words and actions may seem shocking to you as they talk about and treat clients in less than human ways. A youth supervisor in an institution for delinquents said "When I first started working, we had rules that dealt with kids as if they were animals, something you take and throw away. Just lock them up and forget about them." A psychiatric aide recalled that he was told to treat patients as normal people, but he saw most of the staff treating the patients as though they were little children. In your work, you will probably see behavior that will repulse you; it may encourage you to do something to change what is happening right away. These next examples may seem dramatic, because the abuses they describe are easy to see and are results of a system that processes large numbers of people. In such a system, some people are neglected and abused. A psychiatric hospital nurse reports the following:

> A patient had fallen off his bed and hit his head. He was dead the next day when they found him. What happened was, when they made the morning head count, they looked around casually and couldn't find him. They made out a report saying that he was missing from the ward. That day they didn't find him. At 5:00 P.M. they made another report saying that they couldn't find him and he'd run away. The next day, the morning shift came and checked off that he was not on the ward because he had run away. Sometime in the afternoon, they found him by the side of the bed dead . . . in the pool of blood. And they called me and another guy to move him. All the blood had matted and he had rigor mortis.

A newly hired correctional officer described the following experience:

> About four of us officers and two lieutenants were taken back to the segregation area and told an inmate had grabbed an officer in charge of the segregation area, taken his cigarettes and his glasses, and that we would have to go into his cell and get these materials out. When we got to the man's cell, they gave me a blanket and told me that the lieutenant would go in first, hit the inmate in the stomach, and try to tackle him, and that I would throw a blanket over the man's head and we would try to restrain him this way. We took off our glasses, ties, and hats, and went into the man's cell. I remember feeling anxious and scared about what was going to happen. I really didn't know what I was supposed to do. The inmate was backed up into the corner of his cell, and so, as the gate [door] was opened, it was somewhat dark in the cell. As the gate was opened, the lieutenant ran in. I ran in behind him and [tried to] slip the blanket over the man's head—he happened to be about six foot five. I could neither reach his head nor throw the blanket over it. I tried my best, finally dropping the blanket and grabbing the man by the head. We pulled the man down and we had him restrained to where we could get the material from him, but this was not enough.
>
> The next few minutes in that cell made me very, very sick for about a day afterwards. I saw the lieutenant, who had been working with me on the night shift. As we were holding the man, he came with a blackjack in his hand and proceeded to beat the man on the head seriously, accidentally hitting me several times. The man's [lieutenant's] eyes dilated, and he seemed to thoroughly

enjoy hitting the inmate. Finally, another lieutenant had to pull him off. The inmate all the time was hollering "Quit—please, I quit. Don't hurt me." When we left the cell, the man was laying on the floor, and I had a severe stomachache.

A psychiatric aide described an experience in which a patient jumped on him:

Other staff hurdled the patient off and started hitting him and told me to hit him. The patient just looked around. You could have hit him all day and he wouldn't have done anything. I took him to bed and I put him down. Then I saw another employee hit him real hard, and the guy went down and hit his head against the bed. He got a big cut on his head and had to call the doctor to get stitches. He was walking with a limp. They said that he fell over and hit his bed.

A new prison guard reported the following experience:

I was called to the segregation department, where an inmate who had been causing a disturbance refused to come out of a cell. A White man was in segregation with a group of Blacks and had been calling them names and threatening them. He wasn't able to get to them nor they to him, but it was causing total frustration within the unit. The man had to be moved into a quieter segregation area, where he could not hurt someone or tear up his cell. When we went to get him, he had a paper sack over his head, but cut open so he could breathe. He knew that we would be coming in with mace. The captain tried to talk him out. The man refused and backed into the corner of his cell, holding a broom handle, and told us we'd have to take him out. The captain again tried to reason with the man, but to no avail. He then sprayed him with tear gas mace until the man pulled off the paper sack. He [the captain] sprayed some more, but this didn't stop the man. When we opened the cell to go in, the captain and the lieutenant went in. It was one of our more violent lieutenants. He got just clipped with the broom and he backed off. The captain tackled the inmate, and I grabbed him by the head. I got the inmate down on the bed, and he gave up immediately. The captain and I were covered with tear gas, and it made it very hard for us to see. We got the handcuffs and the lead chains on the inmate and put the chain between his legs and led him out of the cell.

After we got him out on the gallery, the lieutenant grabbed the inmate by the hair and hit him five to seven times in the face. The captain and I stood there. Nothing was said. When he stopped, we took the inmate to isolation and put him in another cell. Then I had to make a written report. Also, the captain and lieutenants had to make a report on what happened in moving the inmate. I was told by the captain to write "minimum restraint was required in order to subdue and transfer the inmate from the segregation to the isolation unit." I wrote what I was told to write but informed the captain that, if anything of this sort would ever happen again, my report would read that unnecessary violence had taken place. I was never called on another job such as this, nor do I know whether it has ever occurred since then.

A new employee in a mental hospital recalled the following experience:

The patients have breakfast at 7:45 A.M. After breakfast, they had nothing to do. We had to drag some of these patients out of bed, and I thought it was cruel. But, when I did try to talk to the supervisor about this, she said that these patients must be treated as normal people. It was generally ignored that even normal people would like to sleep late on days when they had nothing to do. A number of times, some of these patients would be hard to wake up in the morning, and they would lose their privileges. Later on, while working on the afternoon shift, I found out the reason why some of these patients were hard to wake up. They were being given more sedatives than prescribed by the afternoon shift. It was a habit among the afternoon shift to keep patients out of their hair by overdosing them with sedatives.

Why isn't something done? How could I, as a professional, allow these things to happen and not try to correct them? Why don't I publicly expose the people involved? A young psychologist related the following experience:

While working at a state hospital for the mentally retarded, I noticed a young man who did not appear retarded. After reviewing his past history and current test results, it appeared that he simply never had the opportunity for any sort of formal education. His initial admission was due to a physical reason and had resulted in ten years of care, but with no regard to his intellectual development. I submitted a short report stating his past and present circumstances and requested that immediate action be taken to begin his education. It was submitted through "proper channels," but, before anything beneficial could be done, it was turned into a press release by an overreacting employee. The press coverage was hardly flattering and served only to embarrass the resident and the institution and create several uncomfortable moments for myself.

An expose' of an isolated incident seldom results in an improvement of treatment. Incidents such as these will force you to make a moral decision. What will you do if you see clients being abused, brutalized, hurt, or damaged?

The Urge to Change the Organization

The agency or organization for which you work has norms—some of which you understand by now. Perhaps you find that you want to change some of those norms. Remember, it is a big, complex bureaucratic organization, and it is very difficult to change, even if you have all the information you need. You were probably hired because you're bright, dependable, and showed some leadership potential. These same traits can lead to your dismissal. Trading your job and a future opportunity for a chance to change the organization is a big decision. Before you make your decision, read Chapter 6.

The incidents described here each represent a brief period in the lives of the clients. A few of the incidents involved several minutes of their lives. Our society tolerates these kinds of activities, largely because the clients are powerless and the abuses are private. Moreover, when such activities are exposed, does the public believe the convict or the warden? The hospital director or the incoherent patient? These clients ended up in the incidents that were described through a series of events. The prisoner in solitary confinement is not a first offender. The mental patient who gets the shot to make him quiet was not a member of a happy family yesterday.

Things that go unnoticed and don't receive much publicity are things that we easily forget. A dripping water faucet doesn't scream out to be fixed. A teacher who "puts down" students (consciously or unconsciously) day after day in school isn't usually fired for that behavior. As long as clients are "killed" slowly and intermittently, nobody seems to be disturbed. A schoolteacher, discussing the results and consequences of achievement testing, described the following incidents:

> For the English teacher, the most important score is the reading score. This score is used to place the student at a reading level of his vocabulary and comprehension. The average reading level of an incoming freshman should be 9.0 [ninth grade]. If the freshman has a 5.6 score, this means that the freshman is reading at the level of a person who is a little over halfway through the fifth grade. Likewise, an 11.0 reading level would suggest a proficiency in reading equal to a student who had almost finished the eleventh grade in high school. Two instances concerning reading scores

remain etched in my mind. The first instance was slightly amusing, the second extremely unfortunate.

The first instance concerned a boy in my seventh-hour class. He was alert, articulate, and intelligent, and I was unable to correlate this with his fifth-grade reading level. Although this puzzled me, I didn't have time to solve the problem, since he was quickly extricated from my class and placed in the seventh-hour reading clinic. In a few weeks he returned. In that short time, he had mastered all the reading skills and was retested by the reading teacher. His reading level was over twelfth grade. Ironically, he turned out to be the most prolific reader in the class.

The second reading-score problem concerned a girl in my second-hour English class. Her test results were average. Consequently, I was surprised when she could not even come close to passing what the majority of students considered an average test. As she continued to fail the tests, I postulated that she was: (A) boy crazy, (B) apathetic, (C) bored to death by English class, or (D) all of the above. My somewhat boggled mind finally arrived at the conclusion that she could not read properly. Unfortunately, by this time she had already failed the first semester.

All of us have been students. We have "worked" in elementary school classrooms for about 7000 hours. The crowded conditions, the noise, and the long lines we all experienced would not be tolerated as working conditions by most labor unions today. Somehow, during those 7000 hours, we learned *not* to be enthusiastic about learning. Remember in the first and second grade how difficult it was not to jump up, make a little noise, and wave your hand when you knew the right answer? In the fourth grade, you probably sat in your seat and put your arm straight in the air when you thought you knew the answer. If you were really excited, you might have waved your hand. If you were still responding to questions in junior high, your enthusiasm had probably reached the point at which you raised one arm and propped it up with your other arm, resting your elbow on the desk. The death of curiosity, enthusiasm, and creativity is not a dramatic, one-time event.

Teachers who were educated in a static school system don't really see the small, slow, constant process of erosion. Students who don't, can't, or won't make it through the educational process become probationers, dropouts, inmates, or patients in another agency of the human-service system—a large and complex array of uncoordinated groups of health, welfare, criminal-justice, and educational agencies. One frustrated social worker described the poor coordination this way:

A caseworker with 70 cases couldn't sit down and rap with one person or do any sort of therapy and administer to their other cases. So they would try and refer this case to Mental Health, but Mental Health had no people to go out and visit their homes; they weren't functioning in that way. They were dealing strictly in medical ways with a lot of the cases. So the caseworker tried to find other resources to compensate for Mental Health. They would try to put the children [in foster homes]; they would try to set up a homemaker with the family so that the mother wouldn't go completely crazy; they would try to get the children to a summer camp. The case became more and more complex, more and more diffuse, more degenerative as the basic crux of the problem was not sufficiently met. So these cases just became fantastically complex sagas.

Organizations and institutions such as jails, clinics, schools, and hospitals have the money they need to hire you. They are the places and the agencies that the community uses to help people grow, learn, or change in some way. The incidents that were described earlier in this chapter may seem to support the notion that these organizations are "human warehouses" rather than places in which people receive help. Incidents such as those can cause a new employee to decide that it's time for revolution. Not *all* staff members are cruel, incompetent, and indifferent. Not *all* institutions and agencies are demoralizing. There is cause for optimism. A mental-health technician describes the changes she has seen within ten years:

People were sitting on benches along the walls of the cottage, one after the other. Very many were elderly. There were no comforts that I would think an old person there had the right to expect. The ward was dark and drab, with two or three aides and perhaps a nurse on duty. The patient population was over 100. The dorms were locked during the day, and no one could lie down. The floors were bare. Two days a week they had bath day. I don't know if that means they had two baths a week or they divided patients into two groups and had one bath a week—probably the latter. Patients lined up stripped naked, waiting in line for baths.

Well, this is a thing of the past. The hospital now is to be used as a treatment center for the acutely mentally ill. Much of the housing has been remodeled and air conditioned. Some is quite modern. [As they improve] patients are free to come and go as they please without being stopped by a locked door. Treatment plans are written up when a patient enters the hospital and followed up until the patient is released. Some are even obtaining jobs on the outside and remain at hospitals several weeks until they get used to their new environment and can take the strain of living on the outside.

At another institution, a therapist reports that:

> Less than five years ago, the mentally handicapped residents were living 25 to a ward, which consisted of one huge room with beds and a bathroom. They were locked in this room all day, except for meals. Because of staff shortage, no one could even attempt to teach the residents basic self-help skills. The daily routine closely resembled an assembly line.
>
> Today, through efforts of the legislators and dedicated administrators, these same residents are living eight to a cottage; not a single room, but a fully equipped home with seven rooms, including kitchen and laundry facilities. Adequate staff is present, and the residents are receiving the training needed in developing self-help skills. They are finally getting the opportunity to become the individuals they are.

The Important People

The trend is clear. Clients are finally becoming important in most human-service organizations. The trend may be a new phase or an organizational revolution. Clients are served as human persons. Agencies and institutions are being judged in humanitarian ways. On the other hand, purely economic and administrative values have not been thrown out; they are being tempered by an emphasis on services to people. Some organizations are beginning to respond to their clients' human needs. A few social-casework agencies are even talking about street-therapy programs. Reform schools are beginning to provide real educational opportunities and skill training that is not related to organizational maintenance. Observers have noted that in the past, most institutional training programs were related to institutional maintenance. A security institution for boys offered welding, cooking, barbering, and electrical and carpentry apprenticeships for honor boys. These trades were needed to secure and maintain the institution. Rural institutions used to offer agriculturally related training. Until the late 1960s, dairy herds were maintained in many state correctional and mental hospital facilities.

Clients' Rights

Consumerism is beginning to affect human-service organizations. The customer (client) is beginning to influence the agency. For years, we have had token advisory boards, student councils, and so on, but the present trend seems to be real. Recent court decisions have determined that mental patients have the right to be treated, and that students have the right to be educated. In other words, clients have the right to receive service. An excellent review of court decisions and present practices regarding clients' rights has been written by Schwitzgebel (1976, p. 817), who suggests that contracts be written for service that describe the process and expected outcome of treatment and specify that a portion of the fee is contingent on the success of the treatment.

The increase in clients' decision making power is largely a result of recent trends in human rights and civil rights activities. Social movements affecting Blacks, women, Native Americans, welfare recipients, gays, and children's rights are examples of these activities. Organizations associated with these movements receive legal aid and support from groups such as the American Civil Liberties Union, Nader and Company, and the John Howard Association. Changes in attitudes and laws regarding clients' rights have challenged the traditional paternalism of many large institutions. It seems reasonable for us (on the outside) to support legislation that would stop drug research on prisoners. Massachusetts recently tried to pass such a law, only to have 500 inmates sign a petition against the bill. (One prisoner testified against the measure.) The inmates wanted the opportunity to do something interesting and socially worthwhile! The bill was defeated (Schwitzgebel, 1976, p. 818).

Many institutions and agencies are beginning to see clients as a resource, because clients are becoming scarce. More programs and services are being developed to retain clients, to satisfy needs that the clients did not originally bring to the agencies, and to recruit new clients. An obvious example of this practice can be found in higher education. Many colleges and universities are offering credit for life experiences, courses developed by students, close-to-home residence centers, and concentrated weekend classes.

Former Clients as Staff Members

Today, many former clients are becoming staff members; some people see this as a very positive trend. (Of course, teachers have always been former students, and this has done little to change public education.) Drug-treatment programs staffed, and even run, by former addicts, probation officers who were once wards of the court, and handicapped rehabilitation counselors are part of this trend. These staff members bring a different understanding to the job and are helpful, because they are able to see the client's world as the client sees it. A word of caution: remember the schoolteacher who used to be a student? The typical student did not become a teacher. The typical drug addict does not become a counselor for addicts. These are unusual former clients. They are most likely the ones who "bought in"—the ones who were conforming clients. Although former clients may have a unique perspective, we can't assume that they speak for all clients. A social caseworker described one former client staff member in the following words:

> Joan was a super con artist. She'd look like she was really working her ass off when she was not doing anything, and acting as if she really knew what was going on when she didn't. She was a very intelligent lady, but she was so insecure. She didn't realize that people would accept her for who she was. She had pulled herself up, and her attitude was "If I can do it, why can't they?" So she was punitive to clients. She'd see a mother beating a child and figure that this is a bad mother. She couldn't see that maybe the mother was frustrated and angry with a lot of other things and taking it out on the child. Joan didn't want to work with the mother. Joan and I butted heads over a lot of these kinds of issues, but she taught me a lot about the streets, and for that I'm grateful.

Each client and staff member enters the system in his or her own way. Your clients have histories. You may want to find out about them and consider spending most of your efforts in getting them out of the system. The next chapter provides a historical perspective of the development of human-service organizations. Such a perspective will help you in your understanding of established staff members.

Summary

Clients, students, inmates, or wards are the reason for your job as a human-service worker. You and the clients make the organization run. It's likely that the clients are more experienced in their role than you are in your job. Remember what you and your schoolmates did to the substitute teachers? You knew more about being students than they knew about being teachers. The treatment you receive from clients may resemble the treatment you gave the substitute teachers.

Some staff members may appear to be indifferent, incompetent, or even cruel. The thrill of your new job may fade into "What am I doing here?" At this point, a personal journal may help you to keep a balanced perspective.

Discussion Questions

1. In what ways did you test your teachers' limits in junior and senior high school? What methods did your classmates use?
2. What traits do you dislike most in other people? Which of these traits do you have?
3. What do you feel when somebody you are trying to help uses you? When did that happen last? What did you do?
4. Is it a part of your job to change the personal values of clients? What values should they have?

References

Jacobs, J. B. *The making of a correctional officer 1974.* Unpublished mimeograph, Illinois Department of Corrections, February 1974.

Jacobs, J. B., & Retsky, H. G. Prison guard. *Urban Life*, April 1975, 4(1).

Jourard, S. *The transparent self.* Princeton, N.J.: Van Nostrand, 1964.

Keesing, H. *The pop message: A trend analysis of psychological content of two decades of music.* Paper presented at the meeting of the Eastern Psychological Association, Philadelphia, 1974.

Licata, J. W., & Willower, D. J. Student brinkmanship and the school as a social system. *Educational Administration Quarterly*, Spring 1975, 9(2), 1-14.

Maslow, A. H. *Toward a psychology of being.* New York: Van Nostrand Reinhold, 1962.

May, R. *The meaning of anxiety.* New York: The Ronald Press Co., 1950.

O'Banion, T., & O'Connell, A. *The shared journey.* Englewood Cliffs, N.J.: Prentice-Hall, 1970.

Schwitzgebel, R. K. A contractual model for the protection of the rights of institutionalized mental patients. *American Psychologist*, August 1976, 30(8), 815-820.

Smith, L. M., & Geoffrey W. *The complexities of an urban classroom: An analysis toward a general theory of teaching.* New York: Holt, Rinehart & Winston, 1968.

Toffler, A. *Future shock.* New York: Random House, 1970.

4 The Organization

Modern society has become so complex and its people so transient that neighbor helping neighbor is simply not enough. Few traditional communities remain. When our older relatives become feeble, some of us are able to take care of them in our own homes. Convalescent, nursing, and shelter-care homes take care of older people. Some forms of helping have become profit-making businesses; serious abuses are common, and many are made public. It's easy to criticize the way in which our society has organized the delivery of help. Bureaucratic organization has weaknesses, and it is the subject of much ridicule. No one has come up with a good substitute for bureaucracy as a means of organizing a group of people and, at the same time, checking on workers to see that they are doing what they're supposed to do. Many of the bureaucratic weaknesses that are detailed in this book and in many other places may not be caused by the structure, but rather by the people who operate it.

Institutions and organizations have a life of their own. They stagnate. They reorganize. They breed. They seem to be fed by idealism and cynicism. They are staffed by idiots and geniuses. They are governed by commissions, trustees, and boards. These governing bodies are dominated by people who have become well known (or at least visible) through channels

An earlier version of much of this chapter appeared in "Strategies for Organization Change by Working with Administrators." *Federal Probation*, December 1977, *41*(4), 38–46. Reprinted with permission of business, finance, and law—people who probably view agencies and institutions in terms of debits and credits. Mandell (1975) discusses the characteristics of board members in the following paragraphs:

> When one examines the background of members of the board of directors of a major hospital, college, or United Fund drive, one finds that most of them own property (business executives), serve those who own property (lawyers and political officials), or earn large salaries in a profession (doctors). Occasionally a union leader sits on a board, but hardly ever an assembly-line worker or a waitress.
>
> One could argue that this should make little difference to the actual work of an agency, which is carried out by professionals. Yet the administrator of an agency carries the board's wishes to the workers. Agency administrators may make some policy contrary to the wishes of some board members, but the board will have to be convinced of the wisdom of it before the policy is funded. . . . I am sure there are some agencies in which the professionals are more conservative than the board. Professionals have their own jobs and agency and professional culture to protect.
>
> The Victorian philanthropists could not envision working with the poor as equals. With precious few exceptions, the twentieth-century human service workers and their boards of directors are no different. Top-down elitism still prevails, rather than bottom-up democracy. Yet during the 1960s, people challenged the hegemony of elitists in the social services, and once the people have tasted power, the battle has been joined.
>
> Philanthropy may be the very glue that keeps capitalism from falling apart at the seams. The economist Kenneth Boulding believes that "nonexchange" transfers of funds, such as foundation grants, are essential to the survival of American capitalism. . . . In other words, if there were no charity to mask the gross inequalities of income and wealth, people might catch on to what is happening and get angry enough to change it [Mandell, 1975, pp. 65-66].[1]

The Board

During their meetings, board members spend a great deal of time discussing budgets. After they've approved of routine items, such as the payment of outstanding bills, they begin to discuss other numbers. Maxwell (1973) has labeled this phenomenon *number numbness*. Board members don't deal with

[1]Betty Reid Mandell, *Welfare in America: Controlling "The Dangerous Classes."* © 1975, pp. 65-66. Reprinted by permission of Prentice-Hall, Inc., Englewood Cliffs, New Jersey.

staff members or clients; they deal with numbers that they can count. Numbers about daily population, average daily attendance, numbers of placements, rates of pledge payments, numbers of runaways, and numbers of credit hours produced are of great concern to board members. Comparisons are made between current numbers and those of one year ago or those of last month. Any obvious differences between current figures and figures from past records cause board members to ask for an explanation. The superintendent or executive director is always ready with an answer—usually an answer that has three parts. (For some reason, a three-part answer always seems to be more impressive.) The board then counts more numbers; however, these numbers are related to employees, raises, new hires, retirees, the ratio of staff members to clients, and staff production rates. This is followed by a calculation of operating costs for organizational maintenance. Numbers of vehicles, beds, desks, rooms, meals, miles, clothes, uniforms, balls, guns, and enema bags are topics of discussion. Such concerns may seem unimportant to you; however, careful accounting, which requires counting, is needed to maintain a cash flow and pay staff members.

Numbers are the bases of national, state, regional, and local information systems. For practical purposes, information systems using electronic storage and retrieval equipment are termed *computers.* The current state-of-the-art in computer programming and use demands that most information be in numerical form. When budget decisions are made, those who make the decisions need to justify their choices. The numbers in the information system are used to justify their choices. Those end-of-the-month reports may seem a waste of valuable time; however, such reports link you and your clients to the system that supports you and your organization.

University budgets are based in large part on numbers of students and numbers of credit hours earned. Many states compute university and college budgets based on credit hours earned thereby giving greater weight to those hours as students progress from their first year to graduate school.

One rural mental-health worker put it this way:

> The monthly client-contact report is what keeps the agency going. My report is added in with the other workers', and that is partly how the regional board decides how much money we get. The reports seemed like a pain to fill out. When I first started here, I used to take them lightly and didn't even keep good track

of the number of hours I spent. One day, my supervisor told me that the budget was going to be cut, because the other satellite offices had been increasing their contact with clients. We had stayed about the same. It was then I realized the importance of these reports.

The associate director of an urban mental-service-delivery agency has a "hell of a time" convincing the staff that statistical reports are important:

I used to talk myself blue in the face to the teachers and social workers in the alternative school about these reports. We have a policy that, every time a kid is absent, someone goes to visit their home—to check on them, but mostly to provide tutoring and counseling. It also provides contact with the parents or guardian. Anyhow, I don't know how many times I had told them to report these visits, but they usually didn't. Our school district reimbursement depends upon the average daily attendance. These home visits count toward a part of the average daily attendance. A few months back, we had a real budget crunch, and I was forced to give two teachers notice based upon a declining school district reimbursement.

Since the notices to these teachers, the teachers and social workers have been reporting not just the kids in school but those they go to visit—even if they're in detention. This has made what looks like a 15% increase in our average daily attendance. Now, I've got to check to see if they are fudging a little on these reports.

Simply put, all boards are responsible to somebody—the state legislature, the church, the immediate community, the taxpayer, or the public—and they are held accountable to those people. In their effort to do a good job, all boards need to count numbers so they can judge what is going on in the organization. After the debit/credit needs of the board are satisfied, items dealing with client services are discussed.

It's difficult to evaluate the components of a program by counting. The number of foster home replacements may have little to do with the quality of life for a youthful client. The average daily attendance in school may not be related to what students are learning. Smaller caseloads for probation officers or smaller classes for teachers have not been shown to produce better client results. Crime rates go up when the number of police officers is increased, simply because more arrests are made. In other words, people-changing programs are very difficult to evaluate.[2] The board needs to ask questions such as "Does your organization really do any good for people?" or "What has your organization accomplished lately?" These questions are difficult to answer. Most organizations count people in their attempt to answer. People are counted in case reports, incident write-ups, community placements, and referrals. Most board members lack the time and the skill needed to perform a meaningful evaluation of any human-service organization. One of the major tasks of the top professionals in any organization is to apply complex evaluation designs to a specific organization. Effective administrators report the results of such assessments to board members.

My experience as a member of two boards was both rewarding and frustrating. Board members have good intentions. They usually serve without pay, take time from their jobs and families, and vote honestly. Most of their mistakes can be traced to two facts: (1) most program questions have no right answers, and (2) boards can act only on the basis of available information. They must depend on their professional staff to supply most of that information. It is a fortunate board that has professional staff who provide alternatives based on accurate and understandable information.

All commissions, or boards, include staff members who keep the board informed so that no decisions are made that would damage the reputation of the organization. These individuals must be experts in keeping others calm. Continued budget support depends on smooth operations. Organizational changes are potentially damaging. Some people interpret such changes to mean that the governing body and the staff have not been doing the best in the past. Changes are risky, because new ideas that have not been tested may not work well. Many changes create work for staff members. If changes are to be accepted by the public, that public will require education—a tough job that is often neglected. This is the picture at the top—a governing body of uninformed individuals with a "staff" who want to keep things on an even keel. This is the status quo.

The director of your part of your organization or agency reports to the governing body—perhaps through somebody else. As long as your director runs a tight and quiet ship, the board remains satisfied. This kind of arrangement makes it

---

[2] In my opinion, the most useful book written on this subject is *Evaluation of Human Service Programs*, edited by Attkisson, Hargreaves, Horwitz, and Sorensen, and published by Academic Press (1978). It would be a most useful addition to a professional library.

very difficult to change the way in which an organization does business. The final section in this chapter introduces some strategies for change. (Chapter 6 focuses on this most important topic.)

Some Administrative Types

Every bureaucratic organization has administrators and administrators and administrators. We have come to relate administration with leadership. Many administrators have studied the best means of getting people to do their jobs and running an organization smoothly. On the other hand, administrators have been studied. A brief description of some of those studies is included in order to give you a general idea of this literature. Remember the names of some of the professors who have written about administration; you might impress your administrator by dropping a name or two. Most of these authors begin by dividing administrators into two categories; then they discuss the ways in which these two types of administrators behave.

Etzioni (1965) describes two major administrative types: instrumental and expressive. The instrumental leader needs overt respect, deals well with hostility, and worries about the budget and how it is distributed. Etzioni contrasts this with the expressive leader, who needs to be loved and to be friendly. The expressive leader is less able than the instrumental leader to stand hostility and has a need to maintain a close relationship with people in various parts of the system. Etzioni's work has been followed by refinements of the terms *instrumental* and *expressive*. In *The Human Side of Enterprise*, MacGregor (1960) uses relatively analogous terms—*theory X* (instrumental) and *theory Y* (expressive). Blake and Mouton's *Corporate Excellence through Grid Organization Development* (1968) is based on two extremes of leadership styles: concern for production (instrumental) and concern for people (expressive). Drawing on earlier work by sociologist Talcott Parsons (1955), Guba and Bridwell (1957), of the University of Chicago's Midwest Administration Center, defined an intermediate position of leadership style—transactional—between nomothetic (instrumental) and idiographic (expressive).

Additional detail for each administrative type is developed by these authors, dealing with concepts of power, control, authority, subordinate/superordinate relationships, communications, and human relations. An analysis of this additional information is beyond the scope of this book; however, the concepts of organizational change and conflict management are discussed in some detail later in this chapter. Of more immediate interest are the administrative types commonly found in human-service organizations.

One professional helper describes her supervisor as "just the nicest, most religious, most rigid, most frightened, most old, most mileage-oriented person I've ever met, who cares very much that the papers have to be made out just right." What type of supervisor, manager, or boss do you have? Several types of leaders' characteristics are described in the following paragraphs. Some of these characteristics and traits may be found in all of us, but they seem especially easy to see in administrators.

Cut and Cover. Country folks know what a sickle bar is and how it works. A sickle bar is a hay and grass mower that sticks out close to the ground from the side of a machine. It has a series of fixed blades on a bar that moves back and forth against a set of teeth that do not move. If all of the blades are sharp and none of the teeth are broken, all of the grass is cut by the back and forth motion of the blades against the teeth. The hay falls into a neat pattern in the field. Even if some of the teeth are broken or some of the blades are dull, the hay that is cut pushes over the uncut hay—the appearance of the field is no different than when the hay is properly mowed. Some supervisors cut and cover. The operator of the defective mower isn't found out until it is time to rake and bale the hay. The nursing supervisor isn't found out until the body of the "runaway" patient is found on the floor by his bed.

Please Mommy or Daddy? It is human to want to be liked. Some administrators, bosses, and supervisors behave as if people work harder for somebody they like; a supervisor/ staff relationship should be based on more than that. Respect should be based on performance on the part of both the staff and the supervisor. Many adults are still dependent—they need a parent. Some administrators use this need, and some even go as far as to hire and keep a staff of the dependent type. Staff lunches, coffee hours, and beer after work resemble a family gathering, with father at the head of the table, rather than a relaxed work group. This variation of the expressive leadership style is common in "socializing" organizations, such as schools, churches, and rehabilitation centers. Berliner, who worked in the federal penitentiary in Fort Worth, saw many kinds of administrators in his bureaucracy. He said that the fallacy of this type of administration is the assumption that adults retain pervasive dependency attitudes and believe that the function of work is to please rather than to satisfy more mature needs (Berliner, 1971).

What Shall We Do? Democracy is becoming popular. Participative management is sometimes taken to mean that group decisions are always better than individual effort and responsibility. Even though the majority has often been wrong, there is often wisdom in numbers. Sharp administrators know when key staff people should have influence on decisions—these people have information from the firing line that administrators don't have. On the other hand, administrators sometimes have information that is unavailable to subordinates. Efficient administrators make it clear whether an opinion or a decision is expected.

Staff members who get their "heads bumped" too many times will rebel; the lumps come when they think that what they say really counts, only to find out that a decision has already been made. Said professionally, overparticipation in the decision-making process, as well as decisional deprivation, tends to increase staff dissatisfaction (Conway, 1976).

I Really Don't Like This Job. A friend of mine campaigned hard to be elected as the chairperson of an academic department in a university. Within two weeks after taking office, he began to draw Xs through the dates on a calendar in order to keep track of the number of days he had left in his term as chairperson. Often, these Xs were drawn before an audience. He made comments such as "I can't wait to get back to my full-time teaching." Some people apologize for being administrators by saying things such as "Somebody has to do the paper work." They are very uncomfortable when they have to tell people "no" or "We don't have any money for that." There are probably many reasons for this attitude, but it seems that, in the helping professions, there is a widely held belief that the only people who really make contributions are those who are in a direct-treatment role. It has become very popular to attack and criticize bureaucracy organizations, managers, and administrators. It is difficult for people who have been on the firing line and participating in these attacks on administrators to find themselves as one of "the enemy." Therefore, they need to apologize for their administrative position.

The Super Helper. Some administrators treat staff members as clients. Staff members get the feeling that they are being treated, educated, rehabilitated, or counseled. This kind of administrator seems to enjoy helping staff out of predicaments. Extreme cases of this type enjoy taking care of and doing things for the staff. They seem to imply that what they normally would be expected to do for the staff is a special favor, because they are such concerned persons.

You, My Staff. These administrators act as if staff people were working *for* them. They see staff members as extra arms and legs to do their bidding. Of course, you work under the guidance and direction of your supervisors. They can have you fired, even though they don't pay you—staff members and administrators are paid by the same people. Both groups should be working for clients and delivering services.

The Admiral. Clean, neat, spotless, scrubbed, and *tidy* are the watchwords. The appearance must be "shipshape." The desk and office of this administrator are always uncluttered. Pride comes from massive, cross-referenced index files. Personal cleanliness is almost a fetish. They consume a lot of paper. You will be impressed by their concern for your grooming and clothes.

Mr. Menopause. These administrators can be male or female. They are afraid, fearful, shy, and indecisive. Many of them have been promoted without the needed education and training. From their humble beginnings, they have risen higher than they really think they should be—and it shows.

The Party Line. These administrators are seen most often in the largest organizations. You never get to know what they believe. All that is told you has come from "upstairs." If the staff members read and had copies of memos and orders, they wouldn't need these administrators; they direct when they are told to direct, they supervise on schedule, and they evaluate on the appropriate forms.

The Boss's Job

I do not know anybody who is an ideal boss. The qualities we expect of human-service administrators probably cannot be found in one person. In order to be effective, an administrator needs skills in human relations, decision making, personnel practices, budget management, project evaluation, program management, and planning. Those who come the closest to having all these skills would likely be paid much more in private industry than they would in the management of human services. Administrators are expected to know something about the actual service an organization is supposed to provide. Moreover, staff members expect them to know about their jobs and understand the daily frustrations they experience. Don't be surprised if your superiors seem to have a lot of other things on their minds—they do. As human-service organizations expand, the pressure on the system increases, and the need for coordination and planning becomes greater; however, as the workload goes up and the budget goes down, planning and coordination are the first things to suffer. Your organization's budget is made for one or two years at a time. Your organization's achievements are considered when funds are provided. Planning and coordination do not show results in one or even two years; therefore, few organizations risk part of the budget for long-term planning. Constant financial concerns may be one of the distractions that keep administrators from being more understanding of and interested in staff problems. As the federal government becomes the source of more and more funding, administrators need to keep track of the new agencies, names, laws, and bureaus that control the money. Much of an administrator's time can be spent writing grant applications and proposals to compete for funds.

Assistants

Assistants are important people; they're usually in charge of many areas that can make a big difference in your job. An assistant's responsibilities include ordering supplies, vacation schedules, overtime pay, work records, special time off, and minor changes in routine operations. On the surface, these functions may not seem to be very important, but watch out. The informal power of these assistants can be great. Some of them have worked themselves into positions from which they are able to dispense political favors. If they like you, supplies will come quickly, you will have the vacations you prefer, your promotion papers will be forwarded promptly without important documents being misplaced, and personal leave will be approved.

Administrators value their assistants and ask them for a good deal of advice on decisions that relate to their area of responsibility. In human-service organizations, these assistants are usually what Etzioni would call instrumental types. They focus their concerns on the supply, demand, and allocation of resources to the organization. Often, these assistants act as buffers and take the heat off the boss—they are the administrators who tell you "no." Instrumental assistants are likely to make their bosses look good. With assistants of the instrumental type, the big boss may be mistakenly viewed as more accommodating and less able to withstand conflict than is really the case. The boss may appear to be an expressive leader who is concerned about the social and emotional needs of the staff. Be careful. It has been my experience that administrative assistants reflect the attitudes and values of their superiors.

Administrative assistants may seem to be evasive when you ask them questions. Remember, they aren't the boss, and they don't make decisions openly for which the boss would be responsible later. They may be evasive in their answers, even though they know what the boss plans to do or what the boss would approve of if he or she were asked in the right way. Assistants' formal responsibility is usually very limited, but often their power is great. They occupy a key link in the chain of command.

Your Immediate Supervisor

The link in the chain of command who is closest to you may have a lot to do with your present job satisfaction and your future career. Take a very close look at your supervisor. You may see your immediate supervisor as a boss. Be aware that the department chairpersons, the ward supervisors, the charge nurses, the team leaders, the lieutenants, or whatever they may be called in your organization, are subordinates— they have many bosses. In fact, they are on the lowest rung of administration in your organization, and they may view themselves as powerless, helpless pawns who are constantly being used by the organization. On the other hand, your supervisor may feel like the most important member of the team. Obviously, your supervisor's feelings about the job will have a great influence on what is thought of you and how you are treated.

Supervisors who have recently graduated from specialized college training may feel important, but they may lack experience. Most of their knowledge may have been derived from books and lectures. Give them a chance. You expect them to treat you with an open mind, so the least you can do is treat them in the same way. It's more likely that your supervisors have had the job you have now or one very much like it. They have probably worked in the organization for a few years and have seen people like you come and go (and probably long enough to see people above them succeed and fail). If your supervisors have been where you are, they may feel they know very clearly how you should do your job. The way in which they see your job now is determined by the way in which they saw the job when they had it. In other words, their perception of your role is based on their personal experience. Your perception of the job will differ from theirs. As a new employee, you would probably be wise to accept the supervisor's view of your job, even though it may differ from the view that was presented by the people who hired you or your own view. Sometimes it's helpful to put yourself in the supervisor's role. What would you do? How would you act toward a new employee? Maybe your decisions would be similar to those of the supervisor. Reserve judgment until you have all the information you need.

After you begin your new job, you should find out which supervisors used to have a job similar to yours, whether they like to be asked for advice, and whether they expect you to leave them alone until you're in trouble. Moreover, you need to know which institutional rules and policies each supervisor openly supports, ignores, or would like to see changed. Another helpful characteristic for you to identify is the supervisor's tolerance for conflict. Is conflict avoided, or is it viewed as an exciting potential for change?

Since supervisors have been with the organization for a long time, they probably have valuable information about the organization that could be of help to you. If you develop a poor relationship with your supervisors, they may not share information with you when you need it. You may be allowed to make mistakes when the supervisors' information could have helped. This will be especially true if, for some reason, you are seen as one of those new employees who won't be here too long anyway. In some human-service organizations, the staff turnover is so great that supervisors have good reason to believe you'll be gone soon. An extreme example of turnover was illustrated by the loss of 300 prison guards in one year at a state prison that employs less than that number at any one time (Jacobs, 1975).

Never communicate to your supervisors that you think you know more about your job (or theirs) than they do. Your tone of voice, choice of words, and posture all communicate a variety of messages. You and a supervisor may say "Good morning" to each other while conveying a number of messages. One "Good morning" may indicate supplication, awareness of subordinate status, or anxiety; another may convey condescension, awareness of power, rejection, or hostility.

You communicate by means of your behavior as well as your words. Most of us aren't aware of the extent to which our pattern of behavior is coming through to other people. Look carefully at the communication pattern you use with other staff members and your supervisors. Fighting with others tends to appear in several guises: in humor, in debate and argument, in semantic quibbling, and in strategy and counter-strategy. Parliamentary procedure provides a convenient structure for socialized fighting.

We all have needs to control and influence others. Advertising, propaganda, guidance, education, persuasion, management, and manipulation are ways of describing our efforts to control the lives of others, to get them to do something that is good for us or that we think is good for them.

Our lives are made more predictable by controls. Formal law is one form of control. When we drive on two-way streets in the United States, we predict that the cars coming toward us will be on our left side. Moreover, our lives are made predictable by a set of natural laws. Physical exhaustion is a result of inadequate rest. Social controls make our relationships with others more predictable. The more control that is present, the less risk for the participants. Those who have the power to exert social control are labeled "authorities." How much authority do you need to have over your clients?

Organizational Control

Control is of immediate concern to those who are in authority. The most powerful tool in organizational control is information—what's "going on" and how it's "going down." In other words, your supervisor needs to know when waves are being made before the splash hits. There are many levels of administration, but all administrators have several things in common. Anyone who has supervisory responsibility has a need to control—to know—and to direct and control others.

Administrators aren't happy when their superiors tell them something about their unit that they didn't already know. For example, it is a bit embarrassing for a prison guard to be told by a lieutenant that contraband has been discovered on the guard's cell block, or for a charge nurse to be told by the nursing supervisor that one of her patients has died.

In addition to control through information, each organization has its own ways and means of control. You know about some extreme physical controls that are enforced in mental hospitals and prisons. All of us were physically and emotionally controlled as children at home and as clients in school. When young children fall and skin their knees, an adult comes and says "Don't cry." Translated, this is a directive to control feelings and behavior. In the view of one young teacher, "Control seems to have become the end rather than the means of good education. To my administrator, control is synonymous with good teaching. The job of the teacher seems to be defined as getting the new recruits to act submissive and to accept control." This young teacher's view is supported by the professional literature. Furst (1975, p. 8) says "School, it seems, is primarily a custodial operation." Willower (1975, p. 219) has made a career of studying pupil control in schools; he concludes that "client control is of paramount concern."

Those who are in authority, who have power to control the key staff, expect you to control your clients. You are on the bottom rung of the formal power ladder in your organization; try to imagine how clients must feel. Who do they control? Whom can they help? Who needs them? What would happen if you gave clients the chance to help somebody who really needs them? I tried to answer this question by giving some delinquent boys a chance to work with geriatric mental patients. The boys, who were "locked up" in a correctional institution, were on the bottom rung of the power and control ladder; the mental patients were in the same position. Some of the results were dramatic. Three boys voluntarily extended their commitment to continue working with the patients. Even the delinquent boys saw a need for control in the hospital. "Two patients got into a fight on the ward. The [delinquent] jumped up and immediately separated them. He put his arm around one and talked to her quietly until she calmed down. He then sat down on the couch with one of them on each side of him and talked to both women" (Russo, 1974, p. 532). Control doesn't have to be oppressive or brutal;

this young man showed kindness and tenderness. Control can be positive.

The Carnegie Corporation supported research at the University of Michigan Institute for Social Research. Studying large-scale organizations, Marcus and Cafagna (1969, p. 127), concluded that "Whether the criterion of a good organization is that of productivity or the intelligent utilization of human resources, the findings indicate that with greater *total control* there is a greater sharing in control at all levels, morale is higher, consensus regarding work is greater, and organizational effectiveness is facilitated."

Control in organizations can take the form of "follow the rules" or "do it by the book and go by the schedule." I have known school principals who proudly display the master class schedule on the wall in their office and announce that they can tell you what part of the subject is being taught right now by Ms. Smith in seventh-grade English. If you act as if you don't believe them, an intercom switch to Ms. Smith's room is turned on. Most prisons and jails are operated like this; those that are modern are equipped with video camera equipment. It becomes especially important to "go by the book" when your organization is about to be inspected, accredited, or visited by outsiders. More about this in the next section.

Organizational Reorganization

Those who administer bureaucratic help-giving organizations use a number of reasons to explain frequent reorganization. Recently, a popular reason was efficiency; today, efficiency is rapidly being replaced by accountability. Whatever the reason for trying to reorganize, there are at least two truths: (1) the most recent reorganization began before the preceding one was complete; and (2) the real reason for all the fuss is to increase control—of clients, staff, money, and organizational norms.

The roles of key staff members don't change as a result of reorganization. They continue to deliver services to clients. They still have a supervisor. They continue to write reports, go to meetings, and have too much to do. Their salary doesn't change. Despite these things, reorganizations can be important to staff members. Keep track of them. Draw them on a chart. Know who your supervisors are and how many supervisors you have.

The formal organization, or the chain of command, is a part of bureaucratic organizations. In Chapter 6, we will see what happens when this chain of command is not followed. The chain of command becomes especially important when things are not going smoothly. One new teacher, who tried to help a student make a schedule change, described the following blunder:

> It was the beginning of the year, and I had this Novels class. The students must be able to read at a junior level, and it's more or less *C* or above kids. I had one boy in there who hated to read and was a poor reader, so I said "I'm going to help get you out of here, because I don't want to flunk you. You could do better on a different level." He said "Okay. Fine. That's all right with me." And I said "Okay, I'll tell you what to do. You go down and you talk to Ms. Adams and I will write a note about how I feel about this." So he came back and he said, "Ms. Adams said that I can get out, but I have to have a note from you assuring the okay." So I wrote one. Within 20 minutes, I received a note from Ms. Adams that said "Report to the auditorium immediately." They were making changes, and all the administrators and counselors were there making program changes, and the kids were lined up. She pulled me back and said "How dare you make a change? I am the only one who makes a change in this program!" I kept trying to explain that the kid told me she gave the okay. I couldn't even get it in until she had got her anger out. And then I told her "But this is just a mistake. The student told me that you had given the okay." So it was just, you know, a misjudgment there, and I was embarrassed—almost to tears.

The response of the department chairperson seems excessive, but students must be kept track of and class size must be controlled. All institutions are responsible for knowing where their clients are at all times. The chain of command includes the flow of this information. Sign-out sheets, roll call, bed checks, and "the count" are all attempts to keep track of clients. The person who is in charge of attendance or the count is usually an assistant principal, an assistant warden, or an administrative assistant.

The Shadow Organization

In addition to the formal organization represented by neatly drawn charts, an informal organization exists in every work environment. An understanding of the informal organization is critical to your survival as a staff member. The shadow organization is the real organization. Groups of people who work together develop relationships, understandings, and unwritten rules; these relationships produce the shadow organization. Much of this book deals with the significant influence that individual staff members can have on the work environment. At times, we all need to punish others and feel good when others are punished, and we have various subtle ways of disguising our need to hurt other people. Setting up a supervisor for the kill, talking through another's remark, using a remark for "innocent" humor—these are behaviors that may be motivated by the need to punish. Similarly, it is necessary for all of us to withdraw at times. We may become umpire in order to get out of the game, volunteer for an observer or secretarial role, sulk, listen, daydream, or use other means of avoiding active verbal interaction with other people. Withdrawal can be interpreted as resentment, ignorance, apathy, or a veiled attack.

Most of us seek support and need to know that others respect us, love us, and accept us. Some people try to keep others at a comfortable distance (withdrawal); others seek to maintain intimacy with a wide variety of people.

Few of us are as accepting of people as we might be. Liking people is not necessarily equivalent to accepting them, and vice versa. When we accept another person, we recognize that person as a human being who has strong needs and feelings, and we realize that we should listen to and understand that person so that effective relations can be established. Acceptance should be a prelude to listening. It's difficult to really listen. Most of us listen only partially to other people; consequently, we often make assumptions about their communications that are incorrect. Listening requires concentration. When we listen, we focus on other people and their communication.

Our individual needs interact with those of our coworkers to produce the shadow organization. Relationship patterns and work norms produce an influence flow and a control system. Remember, the shadow organization is not shown on a typical organizational chart. You have to make your own map or chart. One form of such a chart is called a *sociogram*—a description of social-interaction patterns among a group of people. In addition to drawing up a sociogram, you should conduct some private survey research. Ask the following questions: In what ways do your supervisors' personal values and priorities differ from those of their supervisors', and with which superiors do they cooperate? Whom do they ignore, and with whom do they have trouble? Whom do they influence, and who influences them? It will probably be impossible for you to obtain complete answers to all of these questions— the answers will come in pieces. Some questions will be answered sooner than others. At times, you may think you have all the pieces, only to find out (after you've gathered additional information) that your original answer was either incomplete or wrong. You can get a handle on the "influence flow" in your organization by doing a little research. Roney (1965) has developed a simple means of conducting such research. He suggests that you try to obtain answers to the following questions from each of your coworkers. (Don't call a meeting and pass out a questionnaire; keep your eyes and ears open. You may even feel comfortable asking a few people directly.) The four questions are:

1. From whom do you get advice and information about your job?
2. To whom do you give advice and information about their jobs?
3. From whom do you take orders?
4. To whom do you give orders?

A little counting will show you that there are eight possible combinations of answers to these questions. For instance, staff member A may feel that he takes orders from staff member B, but B doesn't think that she gives orders to A. After you've gathered some of the information (research data) you need, begin to map it. Compare it with a chart of your organization's formal structure. You may discover that the formal organization chart bears little resemblance to the way in which decisions are actually made. For instance, many organizations are moving toward a system of merit pay raises; complex rating and evaluation of employees is used to determine their merit. Each supervisor's recommendations are reviewed as the merit judgments are passed up through the organization. Despite formal, detailed procedures and processes, research has shown that teachers who are "closest" to their supervisors get the most merit raises (Hooker, 1978). This is not to say that staff members who maintain good relationships with their supervisors don't deserve these raises. The point is that the formal rating procedures don't appear to be the most critical variable. It's how well you get along with the boss that counts; not necessarily how well you do your job.

In addition to comparing the formal system of decision making with the shadow organization, you should look at job descriptions. Job descriptions, which are similar to the organizational chart, are usually available to outsiders and new employees. The following examples illustrate the difference between the formal job descriptions and the actual duties of two administrators.

The job description of the executive director reads: "Carry out policies adopted by the Board. Provide leadership to program development. Maintain continuous and systematic evaluation of both program and staff." In fact, the executive director develops policies for the board to approve. Rather than plan programs, the executive director reacts to program suggestions from staff members, develops programs that can be funded, and phases out programs that can't be funded. The major function of the executive director is to keep the financial wolf from the door.

The business manager's formal job description may read in part: "Has staff relationship with executive director. Supervises bookkeeper and clerk. Maintains records related to purchasing, inventory, payroll, and federal and state audit reports." As you watch business managers operate, you may see that they maintain almost daily direct contact with supervisors and collect information from each supervisor on an individual basis. Individuals who have such detailed and up-to-the-minute information can maintain powerful organizational control. After all, most of your organization's activities involve money and, therefore, the business manager.

Another area in which a large difference usually exists between the formal organization and the shadow organization is that of norms. The formal public statements describing your organization and its philosophy may sound something like this: "We intend to be the best of our kind," "We are an organization that is constantly on the lookout for better ways of doing things," "Supervisors really care about the growth and development of staff," and "Ask for help if you need it." However, as you go about your daily tasks, you may become aware of traditions and norms that do not reflect those statements. Instead, you may hear: "People around here tend to hang on to old ways of doing things, even after they have outlived their usefulness," "Staff development and in-service training are of little importance," and "Hide your problems and avoid your supervisor."

Skillful administrators keep careful track of the informal shadow organization as they use it to accomplish their goals. Your awareness of the differences between the formal organization and the informal organization will give you more control over your future as a staff member.

Summary

The new employee usually works the longest hours, has the most contact with clients, and works at the lowest pay rate. These key staff members deliver services; they are the most important staff members. They generate the data, write the reports, and deliver the services that allow an organization to survive. The entire organization "above" these key staff members exists to support the delivery of services. This chapter describes the relationship between key staff members and supervisors, administrators, and governing boards.

The organizational charts, written job descriptions, and other printed policies, rules, and regulations are part of the formal organization. The role and function of the board, the director, the assistants, and the business manager are important to the control and information needs of an organization.

The boss's assistant, or the business manager, usually plays an important role in the shadow (or informal) organization. The shadow organization runs the informal day-to-day functioning of an agency. It's the way things are really done. The identification of staff relationships, traditional understandings, and unwritten rules are critical to the survival of a new staff member.

Discussion Questions

1. Who are the board members of your institution or agency? How closely do they fit the stereotype described in this chapter?
2. How do you judge the effectiveness of what you do with clients? What are your criteria of success on your job?
3. How do you (or would you) relate to the various administrative types discussed in this chapter?
4. If you are reading this book as part of a class, describe how you would teach this class if you were in charge. What would

the consequences of the changes be? If you're on the job, how would you do things differently than your supervisor does? What would the consequences of these changes be?

5. How do you typically relate to authority figures? Describe the various ways in which other people relate to authority figures.

References

Berliner, A. Some pitfalls in administrative behavior. *Social Casework*, November 1971, *52*.

Blake, R. R., & Mouton, J. S. *Corporate excellence through grid organization development*. Houston: Gulf Publishing Co., 1968.

Conway, J. A. Test of linearity between teachers' participation in decision making and their perceptions of their schools as organizations. *Administrative Science Quarterly*, March 1976, *21*.

Etzioni, A. Dual leadership in complex organizations. *American Sociological Review*, October 1965, *30*(5).

Furst, L. G. The educational fifth column: An expanded role for teachers. *Phi Delta Kappan*, September 1975, *57*(1), 8–10.

Guba, E. G., & Bridwell, C. E. *Administrative relationships*. Midwest Administration Center, University of Chicago, 1957.

Hooker, C. P. A behavior modification model for merit U. *Phi Delta Kappan*, March 1978, *59*(7), 481.

Jacobs, J. B. *The making of a correctional officer*. Unpublished paper, Center for Studies in Criminal Justice, University of Chicago Law School, 1975.

MacGregor, D. *The human side of enterprise*. New York: McGraw-Hill, 1960.

Mandell, B. R. (Ed.). *Welfare in America: Controlling "the dangerous classes."* Englewood Cliffs, N. J.: Prentice-Hall, 1975.

Marcus, P. M., & Cafagna, D. Control in modern organizations. *Public Administration Review*, November 1969, *11*.

Maxwell, A. D. Number numbness. *Liberal Education*, October 1973, *59*(3), 405–416.

Parsons, T., Bales, R., & Shils, E. *Family, socialization and interaction process*. Glencoe, Ill.: Free Press, 1955.

Roney, J., Jr. A case study of administrative structure in a health department. *Human Organization*, Winter 1965, *24*(4).

Russo, J. R. Mutually therapeutic interaction between mental patients and delinquents. *Hospital and Community Psychiatry*, August 1974, *25*(8).

Willower, D. J. Some comments on inquiries on schools and pupil control. *Teachers' College Record*, 1975, *77*(2), 219–230.

5 Your Coworkers

Established staff members have grown accustomed to the status quo. The way in which they follow procedures and relate to clients and supervisors fits the norms and traditions of the organization. New staff members' training may have included an introduction to the professional norms that influence and control staff/client relationships. All staff members have been clients in help-giving organizations: it is likely that they have been students and medical patients. They have had an opportunity to observe the norms that operate in schools and medical hospitals. However, few new staff members are familiar with the specific norms that will control and influence their relationships with the organization and the established employees.

The process of staff recruitment, hiring, training, probation, supervision, and evaluation is designed to protect the status quo of the organization. Whatever form the screening process takes, however, it is justified as a protection of client welfare. The people who do the screening are "successful" in the traditional sense of the term—they have jobs, power, and a great deal of control. Hoffer (1967, p. 102) observes that "It is not usually the successful who advocate drastic social reforms, plunge into new undertakings in business and industry, go out to tame the wilderness, or evolve new modes of expression in literature, art, music, etc." Hoffer goes further and says that the misfits in the human race try to fit in by changing the world, rather than themselves. These responsible revolutionaries are the type who were, and are, pioneers—the courageous misfits. An exaggerated example of this type is the individual who has failed in mundane, everyday affairs and reaches out for the impossible. (When people fail to do the impossible, they have much company.) Teachers see this phenomenon in nonreading elementary students who aspire to careers in biophysics or space exploration. To return to the point, the elimination of pioneer types is one part of the selection process that helps to maintain the status quo.

Most staff recruitment is based on lists of job seekers who have met minimum qualifications and who have achieved an above-average score on a battery of tests—even though the test results may have little relationship to eventual performance on the job. In 1975, Menges documented that "Predictive validity of the tests has not been established" (p. 201). He concluded that, even if we could define good practice and professional ethics in various fields, it seems unlikely that these would be related to test scores. Usually, those who get as far as an interview do not behave in radical ways—they want to be hired.

Probationary reviews are intended to weed out incompetents and any new staff members who are causing trouble. New employees who "cause trouble" may not do so by choice. Each of us has built a number of selves to be used in various situations (Goffman, 1969). The way in which we behave with the Sunday-school teacher differs from the way in which we behave with our best friend. We present ourselves in one way to our lovers and in another way to our children. Our supervisors are presented with a self that differs from the self we present to our subordinates. In the life-long process of socialization, we learn various rules of conduct, values and attitudes, and desirable behaviors through which we fulfill our social obligations. These patterns of behavior become a part of us; therefore, to a large extent, we are not fully conscious of the "choices" we make as we enter a new social situation, such as a job. Yet, if we make the wrong choice, the mistake is immediately brought to consciousness. No support comes from others. We feel a loss of face. The wrong combinations of patterns chosen at the wrong time can produce trouble for the new employee and the organization.

Usually, the new employee who survives probation is neither a naive radical nor an incompetent. As a result, the people who are employed by bureaucratic helping organizations are not prepared to sacrifice their income for a principle of justice, fair play, or efficiency. These are people who are employed by an organization that has developed a satisfactory reputation over the years and an image that has allowed it to survive and perhaps flourish. When money is tight, a good solid organizational image is especially important—it ensures continued budget support. Moreover, many people are afraid to change goals and ways of doing business. You constantly hear "This is the way we have always done things around here," or "Oh, we can't do that. It's too risky."

As a new employee in a human-service organization, you may see conflicts between what ought to be and what is. Almost all of us want things to be the way we feel they ought to be—we want to improve them. We want change. You will be frustrated by the discrepancy between the services a client needs and the services you are supposed to deliver; this frustration is felt by every new employee. Many employees in your organization have tried to make changes. As you look around, it's clear that very few of them were effective in their efforts. However, some of them have been successful, and a small number of established employees continue to try to improve the organization. This small and almost invisible minority will be difficult to identify, unless you're a very careful observer. They are not loud and boisterous. They may seem to be plodders. But a few of them have been successful in making what they consider to be important changes. These employees have been rewarded by an occasional success, and they continue to try. However, a majority of employees have never tried, or they quit trying because they didn't experience an occasional success. Some employees become so frustrated by the lack of changes in the organization that they quit. Others stay on and adapt in their own way to living within boundaries at the cost of losing almost all initiative. Research in this area repeatedly confirms that organizational climate has a greater impact on employee satisfaction than actual job performance does.

Patterns of Adjustment

Consciously or unconsciously, people develop means of adjusting to the frustration caused by conflicting demands: they adjust in order to minimize their frustration. Human-service workers adjust in three general ways: (1) they identify with clients, (2) they identify with their jobs and coworkers, or (3) they identify with their organizations (Friedlander & Margulies, 1969; Lawler, Hall, & Oldham, 1974; Prichard & Karasick, 1973). These categories do not fit specific personality types; they describe various behavior patterns. As staff members change, their behavior changes. You will move from category to category during your career. By taking a closer look at these three general forms of adjustment, you will see that there is a range within each form. Maybe you can think of coworkers who fit one or more of these descriptions.

Identifying with Clients

Reformers see clients' needs as most important, and they try to work to change organizations in ways that will help their clients. They feel that professionalism and unionism are unimportant. These people tend to be vocal in staff meetings. They want to help the client first, and then fill out the forms. They want to stop the bleeding before they determine the patient's Blue Cross number. Most of the established staff members see them as radicals.

Although *innovators* see clients as most important, they realize that their coworkers and their organizations need to be changed. They are active listeners, and when they speak, they ask questions. They aren't loud, and they are difficult to identify. The difficulty of spotting such staff members is documented by the fact that sex, age, and personal attitudes do not seem to predict innovative behavior in staff members in complex organizations. Baldridge and Burnham (1975), of Stanford University, tested earlier research indicating that young, cosmopolitan, educated people are likely to be innovators. They found that this was not the case in large public schools in both California and Illinois.

Victims feel that they are being frustrated by the system. They tend to fight the organization, and they may drag clients into the combat as allies. The extreme example of this employee type doesn't value either the organization or the standards of the profession. These staff members feel wronged and oppressed by the "evil" of the organization. They have decided to stay and fight, rather than run. They see themselves as heroes of the weak and helpless. In negotiations, these staff members represent the client; the supervisor represents the organization. Skilled supervisors deal with victims on a one-to-one basis in order to avoid attracting an audience of staff members, who might pick up some ideas regarding working the system to benefit the client. This concept is detailed by Wasserman (1971), who also reports that, unless staff members who have chosen this means of adaption can successfully mobilize the support of both their coworkers and their clients, they are forced to leave the organization.

Plodders identify with clients, but they appear to have given up. They never complain. They seem to be good staff people, but no one really seems to know. They have accepted the conflicts and decided to live with them. They deal only with issues over which they have complete control. A teacher of this type may feel that "Once I shut my classroom door, I'm my own boss." A correctional officer who has adopted this form of adjustment might say "When I am on the shift, they do it my way, even if it is different than the way the other guys do it." A security staff in an institution for delinquents says it this way: "When I'm in charge of the wing, I don't have to use lock-up to control the kids. I don't need it. It's just that I do things differently." A casual observer might assume that plodders would feel satisfied and involved if they had a chance to participate in policy making and administration. However, it has been shown that overparticipation in such activities can be dissatisfying (Conway, 1976). It depends on the individual staff member's need to participate and the organizational climate. *Client needers* are the few staff members who depend excessively on clients.

My Job: My Life. Many people are satisfied and fulfilled by their jobs as helpers. This is healthy, and it's the way it should be. A job in which you feel productive and useful most of the time makes life better for you and your loved ones. However, it's unhealthy to use a job as a substitute for living. When your relationship with your clients overshadows your relationship with your partner or your child, you hurt both yourself and your clients. Your helping becomes confused with your own needs; the confusion leads to unwise choices. Clients become especially vulnerable to an increasing dependence on you that, because of your needs, you do little to discourage. It's not because you mean to hurt your clients; it's just that it feels so good to be respected and needed. Staff members are especially open to this behavior when a recent event has shown them that someone they cared for doesn't need them anymore. Most people need deep personal relationships; however, the use of clients to satisfy this need is not good for either the staff member or the client. The job histories of many professional helpers consist of a series of short-term direct client-service positions. Their search for a good job looks a great deal like a search for themselves.

Identifying with Coworkers

Staff members can adjust to frustration by identifying with *other staff* (the profession or the union). This identification takes two forms: amateur professionals and established professionals.

Amateur Professionals. These people are unsure of their skills and knowledge. They are unable to deal with their clients and their organization. They haven't integrated their own personal values with those of their profession. Their training and education did not help them to become sure of themselves. They rigidly follow professional rules in order to avoid making mistakes. These employees talk about professional ethics, codes of conduct, and areas of jurisdiction. Rigidity in applying rules, regulations, and standards is their outstanding characteristic. They are often the frantic new workers who have forgotten that the process of growing, learning, healing—changing in any way—is an ancient, complex, and natural process. Stephens (1967) draws a parallel between amateur professionals and farmers. Farmers organize their work; however, once the crops are planted, they grow while the farmers sleep. No matter how hard the farmers work, they must wait for the seeds to germinate. The amateur professional has difficulty accepting the fact that natural processes take time, especially when all the best skills, tools, and techniques are used and all the right rules are followed. Blau (1960) refers to amateur professionals as *local*, as opposed to *cosmopolitan*.

Established Professionals. These people see themselves as members of a much larger and more important group than the organization that pays them. They belong to an organization of like workers. Blau calls them *cosmopolitan*. The union, the profession, or the national organization lies outside the agency. Although their primary loyalties are to these outside groups, they do not reject either the client or the organization. They resolve their conflicts with a "holier than thou" attitude that seems to say "If you people would only listen, my professional specialty has the answers to your questions."

Identifying with the Organization

Staff members can adjust to frustration by identifying with the *bureaucratic organization*. There seem to be as many descriptions of bureaucratic types as there are authors. One of the most interesting articles on this subject was written by Billingsley (1964), who details the differences between functional bureaucrats, job bureaucrats, specialist bureaucrats, and service bureaucrats. For our purposes, we will refer to all of these as *bureaucratic technicians*. Bureaucratic technicians treat the organization's policies and practices as supreme. No conflicts are real to them unless either the staff members or the clients threaten the rules and regulations. They carry out institutional procedures. In any conflict, institutional rules and regulations take precedence over professional standards and the needs of clients. Kramer (1974) studied new nurses in hospital settings and concludes that a superefficient bureaucratic-technician attitude is an extreme response to the conflict between school-bred values and work-world values. She speculates that the conflict between what new nurses have been taught and what they find is so great that, in order to survive psychologically, they reject the ideal values that are causing the conflict and wholeheartedly adopt bureaucratic rules and regulations.

Conformists believe that the organization's policies and procedures are important; however, they also value professional standards. Conflicts between the two are either resolved as quickly as possible or ignored. Conflicts between staff members and the organization are very threatening to conformists; they try to resolve or hide such conflicts as quickly as possible. The conformist is the most common type of staff member; as a result, organizations have the continuity and stability they need to stay in business.

The value of getting along with other people and avoiding conflicts has been pumped into us from an early age. Our development and training have been reinforced by three major institutions: home, school, and church. Parents know what is right for their children. Teachers have the answers. The religious perspective is highlighted by peace and tranquility, if not outright acceptance without questioning. Robbins (1974) goes even further in supporting the notion that we basically fear conflict, hostility, and antagonism in his examination of the traditional philosophical teaching that conflict of any type is bad. Robbins talks about the United States as a "peace loving" nation. "Power for Peace" is the slogan of the U.S. Air Force. It is a tribute to human flexibility that any of us can view conflict as potentially positive or at least as neutral.

Who are you? Where do you fit—reformer, innovator, victim, plodder, amateur professional, established professional, or one of the bureaucrats? Maybe you are a combination of several types. Perhaps you don't fit anywhere in this list.

In this section, we have seen various forms of adjustment to the many frustrations that will confront you as a human-service worker. Your adjustment will, and must be, your *own*. The adjustments that you make on the job won't differ radically from the adjustments you make in other areas. If you are an unhappy person, you probably will be an unhappy worker. If you are frustrated at home, you will most likely be frustrated at work.

Staff Meetings

Most organizations provide formalized procedures by which administrators, supervisors, and staff groups can talk with one another. These usually take the form of staff meetings. Routine matters are generally handled in written communication through such things as announcements, memos, and posted notices. Usually, staff meetings are held on a regular basis. My experience has been that, when the person in charge of these meetings doesn't think that there is enough to occupy the group, information that would have been communicated in written form is reserved for discussion at the meetings.

Throughout your life, you have entered groups. The feelings you experience as you participate in your first staff meeting may resemble the feelings you experienced on your first day of school. There is usually a feeling of tension, because of the unknown. We have each learned to deal with this tension in our own way. Some of us have learned how to feel secure in new situations; we tend to focus on things that are familiar to us and comforting for us to see.

The importance of discovering the norms of the organization was discussed in Chapter 1. Staff meetings have their own set of norms and standards. These norms have been developed over a long period of time. If these norms are violated during the meeting, the group reacts to show that a violation has occurred. Usually, the violator is punished in some way, maybe by simply being ignored. A group without norms would have a difficult time in accomplishing its tasks. You need time to discover what your group's norms are.

Don't get carried away with the content of staff meetings. By *content*, I mean the items that are announced, the policies that are discussed, the cases that are analyzed, and the results of the decisions that are made. If you focus too much attention on the content of a meeting, you will lose your ability to see what is happening and how it's happening.

Process refers to what happens during a meeting and how it happens. Careful observation of the process will give you clues regarding the norms and standards of staff meetings. Who talks? For how long? How often? Whom do people look at when they talk? Who talks after whom? Who interrupts whom? Who responds to whom? What styles of communication are used (questions, claims, gestures, tones of voice, and so on)? Answers to these kinds of questions will help you to understand what's going on, such as who leads or who influences whom. How are decisions made? Are there votes, or does the person in charge of the meeting simply say "Does anyone object?" or "We all agree, don't we?" Are decisions made by consensus? Is there a genuine attempt to encourage opposing points of view? Is conflict appropriate, or should it be handled outside the meeting on a one-to-one basis? Should you be honest with others and really tell them how you feel during staff meetings? Who are the people in the group who take on various roles? Who are the harmonizers—those who want to reduce tension and reconcile disagreements? Who are the encouraging members, who act friendly, warm, and responsive to others by either facial expression or remarks that indicate that they heard the other speakers? Who are the compromisers, who are interested in group cohesion? Who seems to set the standards and the norms? Who plays roles during staff meetings? You can answer these questions only by observing the process, rather than the content, of what goes on during staff meetings.

Most people find it difficult to listen to content and observe a process simultaneously. It will take practice on your part. You can practice by listening. It is very difficult to talk and observe at the same time. There are positive and negative consequences associated with being a quiet listener. One consequence is that it increases your ability to see what's going on. Another consequence is that your coworkers' first impression of you as a quiet person may cause them to treat you as if you have little to contribute. As a new employee, you probably are somewhat tense and aren't sure what your contributions are going to be or how they're going to be accepted. This insecurity on your part may be reinforced by the way in which other staff members treat you for being quiet. After you are more sure of the group's standards and norms, you will have a chance to correct this first impression. It is equally important that you check out your first impressions of your coworkers. Your impressions, as well as theirs, are probably incorrect. You have all become skillful at emotional role playing (Russo, 1965).

It isn't unusual for people to disguise certain feelings in order to conform to a socially acceptable model. When you met your coworkers, did you feel immediately that you would like some of them and prefer to avoid others? Did you find that some people instantly seemed warm and trustworthy, whereas others seemed cold and suspect?

First impressions are based largely on a resemblance to people who have been important in your life. Although such impressions may be quite inaccurate, they operate quickly and powerfully. We don't like a certain person—he senses our reaction to him and dislikes us. He turns out to be as disagreeable as we expected him to be. When we seek out the company of an individual we think we're going to like, the person responds to our interest: we find that we like each other. Our prophecy is confirmed. If we had treated the person we rejected as a promising friend, he or she might have become as congenial to us as the person we expected to like. We have mistakenly interpreted an accidental and incidental resemblance to someone else as our own intuitive talent—a "talent" that is likely to mislead us.

We are particularly misled when our pretended feelings cause us to lose contact with what we really feel. By observing, you may see people who seem quite anxious but claim that they feel comfortable. You might hear people ask questions about which they don't really care. It is not surprising that people who have learned socially desirable behavior can pretend to others that they feel what they don't really feel. For some people, the years of practice at pretending have caused them to lose the ability to identify their real emotions.

Traditional Staff Categories

Nonprofessional, *paraprofessional*, and *professional* are standard labels. These labels do not necessarily reflect an individual's relative worth or competence. The term *nonprofessional* doesn't imply incompetence any more than the term *professional* implies excellence.

Nonprofessional

The nonprofessional staff includes those who are employed by your agency or organization who have a high school education or less. This is the group that is typically unionized and has a standard contract. Everybody in this group is hired, promoted and paid in a very standardized way. The groundskeepers, janitors, maintenance personnel, bus drivers, cafeteria workers, and delivery people are members of this group.

Paraprofessional

The paraprofessionals are those employees who, because of their specialized training, receive higher hourly pay than do the nonprofessionals. This group of staff people must account for their working time; that is, like the nonprofessional group, they are expected to work specific and specified hours. If, for some reason, they are unable to maintain their schedule, there are standard reporting procedures dealing with work absence. Some of the employees in this group may be unionized or belong to some form of employee association. Included in this group are electronics-data-processing personnel, laboratory technicians (below the educational level of the registered medical technologist), purchasing agents, dispatchers, specialized machine operators, social-service aides, mental-health workers, child-care workers, and secretaries. The distinction between paraprofessional and professional employees is often blurred by the pressures placed on organizations to serve their clients; however, those who see themselves as professionals work very hard to maintain the distinction.

Professional

The professional-staff category is composed largely of college-educated or professional-school-trained specialists. Their contracts are generally negotiated on an individual basis, though they turn out to be very much alike. Professionals' hours of work are somewhat more flexible than those of other employees. Until recently, professionals were not unionized, but they belonged to professional organizations, many of which are national in scope (such as the American Medical Association and the National Education Association).

Professionals are trained by specialized units in colleges and universities. These specialized units are usually called departments. Each of these departments has its own identity. Each person who is in charge of a department—the chairperson—has an office, a secretary, and a group of professors to whom he or she is responsible. In order to survive, each of these departments needs to maintain the identity of its discipline. Departments need budgets and students (clients), and they have to show production (student credit hours).

A friend of mine, sociologist Jim Henslin (1976), makes an excellent case that higher education, with its emphasis on production, is becoming more like a factory than an educational experience. Departments work very hard to maintain their identities, even though large amounts of overlap exist between departments such as: psychology, counselor education, special education, community organization, social work, sociology, education, nursing, human development, rehabilitation counseling, behavioral science, urban studies, and human services.

The goal of each of these departments is to train people as human-service workers. As a result of the continuing struggle for survival, each department has developed and maintains a specialized professional jargon. Each has its own way of describing people, their problems, and how to help them. In order to keep their students, departments must believe that their specialty is critical to the identification and solution of human problems. This belief is communicated to students by faculty members. By the time the student is graduated, the new helper firmly believes that his or her own specialty is the most important of all of the helping professions. Moreover, many college departments are staffed by nonpracticing specialists who are somewhat removed from the jobs they're training their students to perform.

Professors project their hopes, fears, fantasies, and ideals to their students. Most professors do this hoping that somehow their students will make changes in the way in which things are done and improve clients' services. However, most professors become confused regarding the difference between "what ought to be" and "what is." Nonpracticing specialists teach "what ought to be" as though it really existed. Students are graduated with an idealistic picture of the helping world, some technical skills, a lot of professional jargon, and the feeling that their specialty is most important. This overemphasis on specialization causes serious communication problems among professionals.

Communication between Categories

Opportunities for communication between and across traditional staff categories will be less frequent, yet less formal, than the communication that takes place within your category. Until people from various categories get to know one another as individuals, stereotypes will be maintained.

An example of a communication problem is illustrated by this quote from a guard in a security institution for delinquents:

> For some reason or other, social workers and psychologists come in and give the impression to a youth supervisor that they are little gods that can solve anybody's problem, which really isn't true. They more or less gave a kid permission that whatever he did was all right for various reasons. They used all kinds of excuses for the kid: that he was brain damaged, came from a poor family, his mother was a drunkard, things like this that to me were nothing but crutches. I looked at it a little bit different than they did, I guess, because I figured that, out of all the kids that *do* live in ghettos, slum areas, the percentage of kids that get in trouble is far less than the kids that don't get in trouble. Quite a few kids out there are making it without being put in jail. It caused problems between the youth supervisors and the professional people. In fact, they threw up kind of a brick wall, and when you throw a brick wall up, you're not helping anybody.

The observation of a psychiatric aide working in a mental hospital demonstrates this negative attitude toward professionals—in this case, a psychiatrist:

> I've never seen a doctor call a patient. I have always heard and had the impression that a psychiatrist is supposed to be a colleague and somebody relating to a patient, but I've never seen that happen. I mean, all that I've seen a psychiatrist do is walk up, open the nursing notes and the medicine charts, and write down "Thorazine, 200 milligrams"—that's all he writes. And then he goes off and stays in his office. I don't know what the hell he does; he

doesn't come and watch. He takes long breaks, whatever, but I've rarely ever seen him work with patients.

If you are among the professional group, I would encourage you to take time to develop relationships with nonprofessionals. For instance, the secretary is not paid to work with clients, but you will quickly discover that she or he influences both the administrators and the clients. In addition, secretaries have more information about what's going on in an organization than other staff members have.

Communication between the people who work in the lunchroom, mess hall, or cafeteria and the other staff members is important. When clients are employed in the food-preparation process, information flows from the cottage, classroom, ward, or cell block to the cafeteria through the clients. This information, like all information, can be helpful, harmful, or inconsequential to you, but you can assume that it won't be accurate and complete. A good relationship between the rest of the staff and the food-processing people can be invaluable in terms of special events, such as Christmas and Easter parties.

At times, client-treatment programs can make use of specialized service-oriented personnel as part of a client-treatment team in very effective ways. A part-time job (and a good supervisor) is just what some clients need. You will see your own examples of ways in which nonprofessional staff members can be important in helping. Many nonprofessionals and professionals seek jobs in helping agencies because they like to help. Others consider their job as something to be tolerated— they wish to have as little contact with the clients as possible. The latter can be damaging to the very things that are most important to clients.

Communication between all levels of staff can make life pleasant and allow each staff member to provide the kind of care and help that should be available to clients. I recall a janitor in a small rural high school where I was a counselor. My office was very close to the boiler room, which was the janitor's "office." One day, shortly after a student had come to see me, the janitor came in and said "I'm glad Henry came in to talk to you. I've been trying to get him to do that for months. He really has a lot of problems, and I was afraid he was about to kill his mother." By talking with the janitor, I discovered that he had been counseling with this student for almost three months; and, to my further surprise, I discovered that the janitor was carrying a caseload of about 20 students. He did not seek out these students. They came to him. He listened. He didn't give advice. He kept confidences. He was a nonthreatening observer of almost all of the student body's activities. It goes without saying that he was one of the greatest helpers I've known.

A public-school teacher recalls the following advice from his student-teaching days:

> Cultivate the right people for friends. Janitors, operators of the bookstore, and secretaries are often more useful than fellow teachers. This tip was impressed on me by my cooperating teacher. Her clean room, chats with the bookstore operators, and conversations with the secretaries were reciprocated by special favors from the janitors (they always opened her room for her in the morning), the bookstore (only she could get book orders for her classes on time), and secretaries (Mrs. Bennett knew everything worth knowing).

One public-school teacher describes her relationship with the janitor this way:

> The janitor in our building is fantastic. That man has done more for me and the people in our area than a lot of our administrators. Whenever there was a problem there, like he saw that maybe there was too much mud on the floor after he'd just waxed, he'd say "Will you kind of watch and . . .," and I said "Sure, I'd be glad to." We thought so much of him, we even bought him Christmas presents.
>
> The area that we're in was made for air conditioning, and it's just ungodly hot, very hot in warm weather. He fought to get us fans. In fact, I can remember, before we finally got them this year he went to the office and said "Hey, listen. Those teachers and students are dying up there. It is so hot that they can't survive." And after school, at 3:00 or 3:20 when you'd get out, we'd sit around the lounge if we had things to do, and we'd wait till he'd come and he'd talk with us. "Well, how was school?" and "How was class today?" You felt like he really gives a damn, you know. Maybe he's just being nice, but at least he is.

A public-health nurse talks about a secretary who has become very powerful over the years, to the point of controlling much of the activity of a public-health agency:

> She'd tell you you can't write any more on those appointment pages—the secretary was telling me this, you know, not the nurse, but the secretary. She almost ran the nursing department. She'd

been there longer than anybody, so she knew all these little things that put her in a position to run the nursing department. So here were people who needed their baby's shots and different things. And when you'd be there, there'd be two or three nurses and a helper ready to work in this clinic, and a doctor and only a few people would show up. At the same time, she'd make people wait two and three months for an appointment.

Secretaries are key members of any organization. They have information about what is going to happen before anybody else does. In many organizations, secretaries control schedules, payroll distribution, staff assignments, and information flow to administrators. The quality of your relationship with key staff members will have a lot to do with how successful you are on your job. A teacher describes a principal's secretary this way:

> She takes a lot of the fighting, arguing and harassment that people direct at the principal. She's a very nice person. She knows what's going on. She knows where the papers are, what needs to be done. I mean, she runs the school to a certain extent, and she is a very nice person to have working for you. Any time that we get a memo and don't understand it, or we want to know something about the pay periods or doing homebound teaching, call Helen and she knows. She knows about travel expense, she knows about how to line buses up for field trips; all these things she takes care of and handles, and she answers all the questions. Decisions that, perhaps, the principal has made but hasn't got back to you yet; if it's on her desk, you know, you can find out.

Secretaries, janitors, and maintenance staff are only three of the many kinds of personnel who work together. Especially in residential institutions, you will find a wide range of formal training and backgrounds among your colleagues. Staff members who have professional sounding titles, such as *counselor*, *youth supervisor*, or *cottage parent*, may be English majors, retired heavy-equipment operators, part-time bus drivers, former company clerks, or fraternity enthusiasts just out of college. For those of you who believe you are specially trained, it will be difficult to understand how people such as this got their jobs. Give these people a chance. You may find human beings with whom you can relate—people who have helping skills that you lack.

Traditionally, the mental-health professions have attracted marginally middle-class people: "The counseling process and its array of associated techniques as represented in the standard textbooks and educational curricula is one which has been evolved through decades of practical experience and research with middle-class clients and subjects . . ." (Guerney, 1969, p. 58). In reporting his study on the socialization of police recruits, Van Maanen (1975) found that the typical "green pea" recruit is a 24-year-old, middle-class male. Typical prison guard recruits are not as fortunate socioeconomically. They are in the same age category as the police recruits, but few of them went to college, and more than one-half were "laid off" from their previous jobs.

Socioeconomically, most social workers, teachers, counselors, mental-health workers, police officers, and clergy have been socialized as middle-class people; many clients have not.

Socialization

There are many definitions of the term *socialization*. For our purposes, *socialization* refers to the fact that you have learned all that you need to know in order to get along in the world in which you live. In the middle-class world, socialization includes learning to knock on the bathroom door when it's closed, flush the toilet when you're through, avoid eating from others' plates, and so on. If you learned these things as a matter of course while you were growing up, you probably take them for granted today. We develop many habits through socialization. "Habit is not *original* nature, but something added, as clothes are added to the body. Habit is added to nature by nature—the results of training and experience" (Russo, 1968, p. vii).

As a new employee, you are subjected to another stage of socialization. The organization that hired you wants to make you into as valuable a staff member as possible, and you want to use the organization for personal satisfaction. When the process works well, both you and the organization gain. You are, or soon will be, subjected to "adult socialization," or "acculturation," by the organization (Schein, 1971, p. 401).

Before we examine some studies of the institutional-training process, or socialization, it will be helpful to understand the relationship between norms, controls, and socialization. In the first chapter, norms were discussed. You will recall that norms are unwritten rules and guidelines that nobody really has to talk about; everybody understands them. Although norms are unwritten rules, some formal written rules may be related to norms. Take the simple example of the rule that tells you that you are to report for work at 8 A.M. That rule is probably written down somewhere; however, the norm could differ from the rule. For instance, you may find that 8:20 A.M. is the latest acceptable time to arrive, and that 8:20 to 8:40 is coffee time, rather than work time. This is common in many one-shift organizations. Organizations that operate multiple shifts seven days a week—*total institutions*, as Goffman (1961) calls them—may have a different norm for the 8 A.M. written rule. The 8 A.M. shift may be expected to be on the scene no later than 7:45 A.M. The 15-minute overlap may be used to effect a transfer of information from one shift to another.

In a small way, the extent to which you conform to norms regarding arrival time reflects the extent to which you have been socialized. What made you accept this norm? What controls affect you? Controls exert pressure on you to conform to the rules—to become socialized. At times, controls take the form of sanctions and punishments. In my experience, the controls on staff members who get to work too early do not fit a pattern, and, in some cases, being early doesn't violate any norms. Check it out, though; by arriving early, you might gain first-hand knowledge of some controls! Violation of the arrival-time norm on the late side always elicits controls of some sort, ranging from a bad look to a reduced paycheck.

This rather simple example demonstrates the relationship between controls and norms. Said another way, "The function of all control must be normative, i.e., to define, maintain, establish or re-establish norms" (Millham, Bullock, & Cherrett, 1972, p. 410). Millham and his associates provide a good description and explanation of various forms of control. Institutional control, control by orientation, informal control, and structural control are a few of their interesting categories. For those who work with clients in highly controlled situations, these authors offer ideas that may be of great material value. Each organization determines its own controls and the effects of those controls. Although it is risky at best to generalize to you and your organization, a few occupational specifics of this socialization stage—control—are discussed in the following paragraphs. Again, a word of caution—do your own research on your own organization.

The Socialization of Social Workers

Social workers and social-work agencies have a wide variety of names and functions, but they all have at least two things in common—paper forms and limited funds. The work socialization of social workers includes two seemingly contradictory attitudes regarding paper work. Forms and other paper work are discussed as though they are boring and useless—as though they interfere with the helping process to the point of dehumanizing the clients. On the other hand, office routines, such as filing and keeping records, are highly valued. One explanation for this apparent contradiction is that even the most committed workers sometimes find themselves emotionally drained by excessive contact and use the escape into bureaucratic paper work to preserve their own mental health (Wasserman, 1971).

Since organizations have limited funds, decisions regarding allocation are determined by detailed sets of rules. Most new human-service workers are surprised to find that they are advocates of their clients when dealing with their supervisors. You, the worker, are trying to get all the help you can for your client. Your supervisor is trying to protect the agency's budget. To help your clients, you need to learn to "work the system" in some questionable ways. You may overlook a client's part-time job, or report that a child has a behavior disorder so that his or her family can collect a few additional dollars of support.

The press to accept these kinds of attitudes can lead to an uneasy feeling of guilt (associated with "unethical" behavior) or frustration (if you follow the rules). "The social worker in such a bureaucracy is caught up in this brutal intersection of contradictory values" (Wasserman, 1971, p. 95).

This description of the socialization of social workers confirms the early research of such people as Francis and Stone (1956) and Green (1966). In a detailed case study of a social-work organization, Francis and Stone found that, contrary to classical theory, "The evidence in one area after another did not sustain the notion that bureaucracy implies impersonality and rule-following" (Francis & Stone, 1956, p. 13). Francis and Stone reported that, although rules were seen as impediments in the way of service to clients, if the workers felt that the clients did not deserve more, the procedures and office rules were used to support the workers' judgment. This was especially true of social workers who felt that hard work and an honest day's labor is more worthwhile than homemaking. While a student in the School of Social Science Administration at the University of Chicago, Green (1966) wrote a paper describing the conflicts created within social workers by the organizations that pay them. Although he didn't use the term *socialization*, Green detailed a variety of pressures and choices faced by the new social worker, including the careful evaluation of anticipated rewards and their sources—the profession, the clients, the agency, or the community. Unless you watch carefully, such choices may be made for you by other staff members as they do their part to socialize you.

The Socialization of Teachers

Since the days of the one-room schoolhouse, teachers have been subjected to an intense socialization process. Along with the home and the church, the school remains one of society's major means of transmitting its culture to its youth. In our era, in which many traditional values are being questioned, teachers are caught in a series of value cross-fires. For example, the Sierra Club is supporting values that place the environment before profit. One of their goals is to encourage teachers to adopt this value. On the other hand, teachers are subjected to the traditional view that a capitalistic system depends on profit. This latter view maintains that the goal of public schools should be to increase the productive capacity of young people by helping them to develop social skills, technical competencies, and motivations that are appropriate in a capitalist society. Bowles and Gintis (1976), of the University of Massachusetts, claim that the purpose of public schools is to legislate inequality and perpetuate the expropriation of the products of labor as profit for stockholders. These kinds of value decisions will confront the new teacher as a part of the socialization process.

Of all the helping professions, teaching has been studied most intensively in terms of the socialization process. The literature on the socialization of classroom teachers can be placed in four categories: early childhood experiences, the influence of important models, peer influence, and students as socializing agents.

The psychodynamic process begins early in the future teacher's life. Ben Wright, the leading exponent of this position, even discounts the student-teaching experience as simply a continuation of the early fantasy-like ideas regarding teaching (Wright & Tusha, 1968). In a series of articles, Lortie (1966, 1968, 1969) argues that some pupils become teachers as a result of childhood experiences. Lortie claims that the potent models of teachers are internalized by their students. One of the characteristics of effective models is that they possess power. Teachers certainly possess power over children. Smith and Geoffrey (1968) describe a teacher's own personal belief system and its influence on classroom behavior. As one reads Smith, it is apparent that he is discussing the influence of early experiences with teachers that the novice teacher displays in his or her own classroom behavior (pp. 49–50). Smith emphasizes the socialized belief, at least at the elementary level and in high school athletics, that pupils "belong" to a teacher and have a responsibility to that teacher for their behavior, even when they are not with that teacher. This belief has been passed on from generation to generation and has apparently become a part of the school culture.

The socialization effect of other teachers and supervisors is powerful, because they are what Edgar and Warren (1969) call "sanctioning colleagues." A sociological study conducted by Lortie (1975), *School Teacher*, details the socialization pressure on new teachers with special emphasis on the first year of teaching. In partial agreement with Edgar and Warren, Lortie reports that new teachers turn to other teachers for informal exchanges of opinions and experiences (p. 72).

Haller (1967) supports the view that the most powerful socializing agents for teachers are students. The influence of children on the process of making a person a teacher is evident to me each time the local kindergarten teacher talks to me as though I were five years old. She has adopted the language and much of the other social behavior of her kindergarten students.

The Socialization of Nurses

Nurses, like teachers, are semiprofessional, in the sense that they are employed on rather standard contracts. Nurses and teachers also are similar in that they "tend to have horizontal occupational structures located in vertical multilevel organization hierarchies" (Alutto & Belasco, 1974, p. 226). In other words, chances for advancement in an organization are slim for teachers and nurses. The characteristics needed for advancement to administrative positions differ from those that make a good teacher or nurse. This absence of professional advancement opportunities encourages many teachers and nurses to leave their professions (Alutto & Belasco, 1974; Kramer, 1974). Within two years after graduation, almost 30% of nurses leave the occupation (Kramer, 1974, p. 29). Over 70% of male teachers intend to leave the classroom (Lortie, 1975, p. 87), and women see their continued teaching as contingent on events in their lives outside their occupation (Lortie, 1975, p. 99). In both teaching and nursing, the career system favors recruitment into the profession, rather than retention. This practice results in low personal involvement and commitment on the part of large numbers of professional people in these fields. Like all socializing agents, these low-commitment types will encourage new employees to accept and adopt their views, attitudes, and norms. Remember, low-commitment employees see an informal shadow organization that differs from the shadow organization seen by dedicated and committed employees.

Those of you who plan to be nurses will see a contrast between low-commitment R.N.'s and high-commitment L.P.N's and aides. Kramer (1974) describes the socialization role that aides play with regard to new R.N.'s. Many new nurses are surprised to find that these aides have so much experience and knowledge about the organization. (For new nurses, Kramer's book is worth reading.) My experience as a teacher tells me that the same is true of school secretaries, cafeteria workers, and custodians. As I said before, these nonprofessional people can help to make or break a new employee.

The Socialization of Police Officers

Police officers, like nurses, teachers, and social workers, are faced with many decisions in the course of a day's work. Often, the decisions that police officers make border on choices that technically should be made by judges and juries. Most police recruits, or "green peas," are highly motivated and committed to the department (Van Maanen, 1975). They want to be effective members of the team and enforce the law according to their academy training. This high commitment of police recruits is in vivid contrast to new "fish," or new prison guards, who view their careers as a long series of temporary jobs (Jacobs, 1974). Police recruits are subjected to "the speedy and powerful character of the police socialization process resulting in a final perspective which stresses a 'lay low, don't make waves' approach to urban policing" (Van Maanen, 1975, p. 207). In fact, officers who clung to high expectations were found by Van Maanen to be least likely to be evaluated as good police officers by their sergeants, whereas those with the least favorable attitudes were rated as better performers.

The initial high team spirit of police recruits is refined by the socialization process once they become members of squads. The members of each squad are assigned a specific geographic area; they are expected to back one another up, cover for one another, and share the work load. New officers who are "too committed" can create additional work for other squad members—not a good way to win friends.

Socialization in Human-Service Occupations

Six general points can be made regarding socialization in human-service occupations. These points relate to educational preparation, the sequence of socialization events, the identification of new employees, the probation period, trainers, and the "no rat" rule.

Educational preparation. Your educational preparation (academy, college, orientation sessions, or training programs) may or may not be useful in your new job as a human-service worker. Some of what you've learned in school won't fit. This is the real world you're in now.

The sequence of socialization events. The sequence of socialization events begins with the recruitment process and ends with either termination or successful socialization. These events serve to maintain the status quo in an organization.

The identification of new employees. New uniforms, special classes, and crowded offices are a few of the physical characteristics that tell the established employee you're new on the job.

The probation period. The longer the probation period, the more demanding and degrading it can be. During this test period, your socialization will be evaluated by your trainers, coaches, and managers. They will determine your success on the basis of your acceptance of the norms, standards, and attitudes that keep the organization running as it has always run. You will know whether you've failed in your socialization efforts—the result of failure in this area is isolation.

Trainers. Professors, teachers, instructors, and preceptors are all trainers. On your new job you will have a coach. It is difficult to identify coaches, because they may not be formally assigned to their roles. Your office mate, the teacher across the hall, the aide who works your shift, or a client may act as your coach.

The "no rat" rule. The "no rat" rule is common to all organizations. It is considered risky for any employee to "tell on," "gig," or "squeal on" another employee. It is especially risky for a new employee to rat on an established employee.

Volunteer Staff Members

As a human-service worker, you will be working with volunteers. Volunteers can be either a big help or a pain in the neck. A volunteer program that includes good recruitment, selection, training, and supervision can be a big help to you. Maybe the volunteers can do a portion of your job that you'd rather not do. When volunteers are present, you might do those things that you always wanted to do but never had time. The one thing all volunteers have in common is time to give. When you work with volunteers in a partnership, you might find that you have more total human contact with clients. Moreover, you may find volunteers who have skills and experiences you lack.

The Growth of the Volunteer Movement

More than 500,000 agencies in the United States have volunteer programs (Scheier, 1971). Perhaps you work for one of these agencies or are a volunteer in an agency. Volunteerism is not new; however, in recent years, the idea has caught on. Familiar movements, such as the Red Cross, have been joined by other national programs, such as the Peace Corps and VISTA.

An increased demand for services, shorter work weeks, longer life span, and higher levels of unemployment have all added to the volunteer movement—approximately 50 million adults are involved in some form of volunteer service to other people (Scheier, 1971, p. 1). Agency budgets are being restricted as the competition for tax dollars becomes more intense. Requests for the expansion of paid staff positions fall on deaf ears. Meanwhile, some people have more time on their hands than they ever had before. The majority of these people are socioeconomically middle class or above. They are the ones who volunteer—people who need to be needed by and involved with others. Most of us have a desire to count—to make a difference in somebody's life. As paid jobs become more scarce—especially for college graduates—more and more young people are finding that one of the best means of obtaining a job in an agency or institution is to do volunteer work. It gives them practical experience (something to add to a future job application) and an opportunity to be on the spot in case an opening occurs in the agency in which they are volunteering their time.

Pros and Cons

My experience in four organizations has been that the majority of volunteers are of upper-middle-class status and have significant contact with many community resources through their families, churches, clubs, and friends. Often, such contacts can be used to help you and your clients. It can become a bit sticky when you find yourself supervising a volunteer who is of higher status in the community than you think you are.

Aside from the direct advantages to you and your clients that are made possible by volunteers, the community education and organizational visibility that volunteers provide can help to support requests for new facilities, larger budget, and program expansions.

The specific roles that volunteers have in your organization will depend on the type of clients you serve and the skills and competencies of the volunteers. Volunteers in the field of juvenile probation are being used in roles that range from administrative clerks to diagnostic psychologists (Scheier, 1971).

Let's look at the other side of this issue. Volunteer programs have been troubled by high turnover rates, lack of commitment from paid staff, low volunteer dependability rates, poor record keeping, and bad management in general (Scheier, 1972, p. 33).

Plan carefully, and learn from the experience of others.[1] Scheier (1971, 1972) of Boulder, Colorado, has some excellent suggestions. Additional help is available from Leenhouts (1969), in Royal Oak, Michigan, who entered the volunteer movement as a judge in a state district court.

The Michigan program has the zeal of missionaries as well as good training films and other material. The Colorado program is well documented and provides an excellent description of the potential strengths and weaknesses of volunteer programs.

Most of the weaknesses of volunteer programs concern the following issues:

1. Paid staff believe that volunteer programs reduce their control over clients.
2. The "friend to the client" role of the volunteer can cause conflict with the paid staff.
3. Rather than serve more clients better, paid staff want to have more control over the programs they now have.
4. High turnover rates among volunteers cause problems for clients.
5. Poor orientation and supervision of volunteers is common.
6. Recruitment and selection practices are inadequate.
7. There are too many volunteers, and there is not enough to do.

Even if your organization has a poorly run volunteer program, you may have an opportunity to use the volunteers assigned to you. But wait—don't try to reorganize the entire volunteer program. Do that later. In order to use your volunteers effectively, you will need to:

1. Be specific and clear about what kinds of help you need to better serve your clients.
2. Select those needs that the organization allows volunteers to fill.
3. Determine in which of these needs your volunteers are most interested.

[1] Under a grant from the National Institute of Corrections, the National Information Center on Volunteerism (NICOV) was established as an information service for jails, probation, parole, institutions, and community-based facilities using, or planning to use, volunteer resources. Bibliographies of published and unpublished materials and recommended "bookshelf libraries" were developed. For information, contact: Library Coordinator; NICOV; P.O. Box 4179; Boulder, Colorado 80306. Telephone: (303) 447-0492.

4. Establish a *regularly* scheduled time to meet person-to-person with the volunteers.
5. Be honest—tell it like it is when you talk with your volunteers.
6. Listen—the volunteers may have some ideas that haven't occurred to you.
7. Both you and the volunteers need to make and keep careful records of activities—especially client contact.

Paid staff in your organization may have negative attitudes regarding volunteers. These staff members may have developed these attitudes as a result of experience. Don't argue with them or try to change their attitude. The best way to help them change is to demonstrate the effective use of volunteer staff. Even that may have no effect if the presence of volunteers in the organization threatens them. Some staff members may be made uncomfortable by volunteers who are intelligent and of high social class. On the positive side, suppose that everything the volunteer does and says is good! But wait—are you breaking any organizational norms with your good volunteer program? If so, you need to decide whether breaking the norm to obtain the volunteer service is worth the price that you may have to pay.

Due to the nature of their positions, volunteers can afford to take more risks than paid staff members can. They have a source of livelihood independent of the organization. This is especially true of national volunteers, such as members of VISTA, who don't work in their home communities. Risk taking can be very productive. One VISTA volunteer was responsible for starting one of the first youth-emergency services in my local area. It has now grown to encompass a wide geographic region. A part of this service is supervised and professionally supported by the local mental-health professionals, who take turns carrying a "call beeper" when the mental-health clinics are not open. Volunteers call the professionals when they need their help or counsel with a client.

Conclusion

Many arguments are heard for and against the use of volunteers; however, little research regarding the effectiveness of volunteers has been done. The only well-controlled study I can locate was conducted at the Institute for Social Research (Berger, Crowley, Gold, Gray, & Arnold, 1975). This study concluded that clients who work with volunteers are neither better nor worse off than clients who don't work with volunteers. Unless you are prepared to do such a study or find additional studies, don't make exaggerated claims for or against volunteerism.

Summary

Each of us has built a set of selves for various social situations. Our parents "coached" us on how to behave when particular relatives came to visit. We learned patterns of behavior that have been more or less effective in dealing with teachers and parents. The lifelong process of socialization teaches us various rules of conduct, values, and attitudes, as well as behaviors that we use to fulfill our social obligations. These become so much a part of us that we are not fully conscious of the "choices" we make. When we enter the social situation of a new job, we present the social self that we "choose." This "choice" becomes a factor in the adult socialization process that is about to begin. The organization is attempting to transform us into valuable employees; we want to use the organization for our personal satisfaction. Coworkers play a key role in this socialization process. Staff meetings provide one opportunity for the socialization of new employees.

Discussion Questions

1. What changes would you like to see on your job (or in your school)? Are they important enough to do something about? How much would it "cost" to make the changes? How much is it "costing" you not to try to make the changes?
2. How would you describe the organizational climate where you work (or go to school)? To what extent does this climate affect you and your performance?
3. Where do you fit in the adjustment patterns discussed in this chapter? Are there patterns that weren't discussed? How have you adjusted to your present position—school or work? How much of the "victim" is in you?
4. What forces and models operated in your socialization? To what extent does your behavior conform to that of the significant people in your life?

References

Alutto, J. A., & Belasco, J. A. Determinants of attitudinal militancy among nurses and teachers. *Industrial and Labor Relations Review*, June 1974, *27*(2).

Baldridge, J. V., & Burnham, R. A. Organizational innovation: Individual, organizational, and environmental impacts. *Administrative Science Quarterly*, June 1975, *20*.

Berger, R. J., Crowley, J. E., Gold, M., Gray, J., & Arnold, M. S. *Experiment in a juvenile court—A study of a program of volunteers working with juvenile probationers.* Ann Arbor: Institute for Social Research, 1975.

Billingsley, A. Bureaucratic and professional orientation patterns in social casework. *Social Service Review*, December 1964, *3*(4), 400-407.

Blau, P. M., Wolf, V. H., & Stauffer, R. E. The structure of small bureaucracies. *American Sociological Review*, April 1960, *31*, 179-192.

Bowles, S., & Gintis, H. *Schooling in capitalist America.* New York: Basic Books, 1976.

Conway, J. A. Test of linearity between teacher participation in decision making and their perceptions of their schools as organizations. *Administrative Science Quarterly*, March 1976, *21*.

Edgar, D. E., & Warren, R. L. Power and autonomy in teacher socialization. *Sociology of Education*, 1969, *42*, 417-426.

Fletcher, J. *Situation ethics.* Philadelphia: Westminster Press, 1966.

Francis, R. G., & Stone, R. C. *Service and procedure in bureaucracy: A case study.* Minneapolis: University of Minnesota Press, 1956.

Friedlander, F., & Margulies, N. Multiple impacts of organizational climate and individual value systems upon job satisfaction. *Personnel Psychology*, 1969, *22*, 171-183.

Goffman, E. *Asylums.* New York: Doubleday, 1961.

Goffman, E. *The presentation of self in everyday life.* Garden City, N.Y.: Doubleday/Anchor, 1969.

Green, A. D. The professional social worker in the bureaucracy. *Social Science Review*, 1966, *40*(1), 71-83.

Guerney, B. G. (Ed.). *Psychotherapeutic agents: New roles for nonprofessionals, parents, and teachers.* New York: Holt, Rinehart & Winston, 1969.

Haller, E. J. Pupil influence in teacher socialization: A socio-linguistic study. *Sociology of Education*, 1967, *40*, 316-333.

Henslin, J. M. University as a factory. In J. M. Henslin & L. T. Reynolds (Eds.), *Social problems in American society.* Boston: Holbrook Press, 1976.

Hoffer, E. *The ordeal of change.* New York: Harper & Row, 1967.

Jacobs, J. B. *The making of a correctional officer: 1974.* Unpublished mimeograph, Illinois Department of Corrections, February 1974.

Kramer, M. *Reality shock: Why nurses leave nursing.* St. Louis: C. V. Mosby Co., 1974.

Lawler, E. E., III, Hall, D. T., & Oldham, G. R. Organizational climate: Relationship to organizational structure, process, and performance. *Organizational Behavior and Human Performance*, 1974, *11*, 139-155.

Leenhouts, K. J. *Concerned citizens and a city criminal court.* Available from Royal Oak Municipal Court, City Hall, Royal Oak, Michigan.

Lortie, D. C. Teacher socialization: The Robinson Crusoe model. *In the real world of the beginning teacher.* Report of the Nineteenth National TEPS Conference, Washington, D.C.: NEA, 1966, 54-66.

Lortie, D. C. Shared ordeal and induction to work. In Howard S. Becher (Ed.), *Institutions and the person.* Chicago: Aldine, 1968.

Lortie, D. C. The balance of control and autonomy in elementary school teaching. In A. Etzioni (Ed.), *The semi-professions and their organization.* New York: Free Press, 1969, 1-53.

Lortie, D. C. *Schoolteacher: A sociological study.* Chicago: University of Chicago Press, 1975.

Menges, R. J. Assessing readiness for professional practice. *Review of Educational Research,* Spring 1975, *45*(2), 173-207.

Millham, S., Bullock, R., & Cherrett, P. Social control in organizations. *British Journal of Sociology,* December 1972, *23*(4), 406-421.

Prichard, R. D., & Karasick, B. The effects of organizational climate on managerial job performance and job satisfaction. *Organizational Behavior and Human Performance,* 1973, *9*, 126-146.

Robbins, S. P. *Managing organizational conflict: A new traditional approach.* Englewood Cliffs, N. J.: Prentice-Hall, 1974.

Russo, J. R. Emotional role playing. *Group process: A learning method.* Delinquency Study Youth Development Project, Southern Illinois University, Edwardsville, Illinois, 1965.

Russo, J. R. (Ed.). *Amphetamine abuse.* Springfield, Ill.: Charles C Thomas, 1968.

Scheier, I. H. *Volunteers in court: A manual.* USDHEW-SRS (72-26007). Washington, D.C.: U.S. Government Printing Office, 1971.

Scheier, I. H. *Guidelines and standards for the use of volunteers in correctional programs.* U.S. Department of Justice (LEAA), Stock #2500-00236. Washington, D.C.: U.S. Government Printing Office, 1972.

Schein, E. H. The individual, the organization, and the career: A conceptual scheme. *Journal of Applied Behavioral Science,* 1971, 7, 401-462.

Smith, L. M., & Geoffrey, W. *The complexities of an urban classroom: An analysis toward a general theory of teaching.* New York: Holt, Rinehart & Winston, 1968.

Stephens, J. M. *The process of schooling.* New York: Holt, Rinehart & Winston, 1967.

Van Maanen, J. Police socialization: A longitudinal examination of job attitudes in an urban police department. *Administrative Science Quarterly,* 1975, *20.*

Wasserman, H. The professional social worker in a bureaucracy. *Social Work,* January 1971, *16*(1), 89-95.

Wright, B. D., & Tusha, S. A. From dream to life in the psychology of becoming a teacher. *School Review,* 1968, *76*, 253-293.

6 The Other Establishments

If you are employed by a human-service agency, your experience has shown you that some agency policies and practices don't help either you or your clients. You have seen administration mess up. Perhaps you can identify the staff members with whom you enjoy working—and those you avoid, if possible. Your inflated expectations of your job have settled into a daily reality. As you strive to deliver services, you may begin to wonder whether all organizations are as poorly operated as yours. They can't be, you say—if they were, the system wouldn't work at all.

Since few agencies can provide all the services a given client needs, you will work with other human-service organizations to get help for your clients. Your experience with other agencies may lead you to reevaluate your opinion of your organization.

Referral

You have a client who needs a service that your agency can't provide. Your rules and regulations tell you how to seek referral help. The referral regulations most likely tell you to go to (or send people to) your supervisor. Your supervisor goes to the boss, who then goes to the big boss of your agency, who communicates to the big boss of the other agency, who goes to a supervisor to get a key staff person to contact either you or your client. Often, you aren't told that your client has been contacted; moreover, the referral process has taken so long that you've probably forgotten about the original contact. Even if all of the proper people are notified with a minimum of delay, the help that your client needs may come too late.

"Human-service systems" has become a popular phrase. Usually, when people think of the word *system*, they think of coordination, a unitary whole, and comprehensive assemblage. The problems of coordination and cooperation among service institutions and agencies have not been solved. Like the weather, everybody talks about them, but nobody seems to be able to change them. Each organization has its own goals, procedures, and clients. Each has its own turf. Everybody believes that everybody else ought to change. Even radical social workers are slow to change their methods. For example, social caseworkers are accepting and supportive of protests in housing reform, but they reject client protests in the area of public welfare (Epstein, 1970, p. 127). Despite the fact that poor coordination exists, you have, or will have, clients who need the services of agencies other than your own. You can't rely on the system to secure help from other agencies for your clients.

Efficient and experienced human-service workers have built their own network of agency contacts. These "personal" networks are a logical consequence of the conflict that is built into the system. Many agencies compete with one another for a share of limited government funds. Some agencies compete with one another for office space. Most important, each agency has its own goal—its reason for existing. At times, various agency goals appear to be in conflict with one another, or, at a minimum, act to interfere with one another's service to clients.

Different Agencies; Different Priorities

Individuals who work for a state mental-health agency may be formally concerned about the mental health of all the people in the state; however, they are told that their first priority is to reduce the long-term populations in the state mental hospitals. As a result, the state mental-health agency's first priority is the community placement of every patient it can possibly remove from the hospital. The social worker who works with the welfare department has clients who are not yet hospitalized and need counseling help. Long waiting lists, transportation problems, child-care arrangements, and a concern for their personal appearance at the new agency may complicate the clients' original problems. Therapeutic help for public-welfare clients is simply not a high priority for the state mental-health department. That department is being judged by its ability to reduce hospital populations. The priorities that are directed "downward" from the budget makers to the board, and from the board to the director, affect the way in which each help-giving organization looks at clients. Very real budget problems would result if the priorities imposed by those who control the agencies' money were ignored.

In addition to budget pressures, each agency has its own set of goals for its clients. Most religious organizations are interested in clients from birth through death, with special emphasis on the soul. Much like a vocational-rehabilitation agency, a church's interest extends beyond immediate service to its clients. Both the church and the rehabilitation agency have goals that are longitudinal, or future oriented. Compare this orientation with that of a medical hospital and a probation department. The medical hospital's goal is accomplished when the patient is cured; the probation department's goal is accomplished when the client's time is up. These agencies' interest in clients is less future oriented than that of the church.

A second way to view an agency's service goals for clients is to consider how much of the client's life is of concern to the agency. Organizations that operate residential facilities (*total institutions*, as Goffman [1961] calls them) deal with the entire life space of each client, from moral beliefs to physical cleanliness. Due to the way in which most secondary schools are organized today, teachers may see as many as 250 students each day. They focus on the academic concerns of their students. This narrow focus is a consequence of the crush of numbers; most communities expect a much broader focus. Many responsibilities that traditionally were assumed by the family, such as sex education, personal counseling, and career development, are now considered to be functions of the school. School boards have responded by hiring specialists, each of whom has hundreds of clients. Despite the illusion of concern that is produced, the main focus is academic. When a student doesn't make it in the academic system, agencies that have a broad focus take over. Foster homes, detention homes, and reform schools deal with the entire life space of a client. Public schools and total institutions have differing "lateral" views of clients—one is narrow, and the other is broad (Lefton & Rosengren, 1966).

It may help you to look at the various organizations for which you work in terms of the ways in which they view clients longitudinally and laterally. Much interagency conflict results from differences in these views. The worker from the mental-health clinic who asks the teacher to "understand" a student may be met with "Understand him? Hell, I wish someone would understand *me.*" Many teachers who deal with as few as 30 students per day consider *social work, psychology,* and *mental health* to be dirty words (Smith & Geoffrey, 1968, p. 213). Many workers who deal with student dropouts see teachers' narrow academic concerns as the cause of the dropout problem.

Each organization views its clients in a particular way; this could help to explain the lack of interagency cooperation. Although the social caseworker who provided the following input did not see the problem from this angle, she realized that her client was not being served:

> There was an intake on a child. The parents had called Mental Health and told them that they wanted this particular child of theirs institutionalized. Mental Health passed the buck on to us. It was not our problem. If we had passed the buck back to Mental Health, we would have been in trouble anyway. We couldn't win for losing. So we dealt with the case as best we could and got it to the point where we gave this woman enough resources to effectively deal with Mental Health so that she could get some action from them. It took several hours of our time. That's one way I learned that Mental Health wasn't functioning, and on a primitive level. Then, in another case I had, the caseworker had actually referred the woman to Mental Health. The woman wouldn't go to Mental Health, because she was afraid to leave her house. She was that sick. So we got the kids out of the house. We did that. But Mental Health is supposed to have resources, as I understand it, for visiting caseworkers or visiting therapists. There was no such resource available. Mental Health was also supposed to have resources for transportation. It didn't. So I would go and sit and talk with this woman and try to help her.

Her clients were not being served by the mental-health agency in ways that were efficient and helpful. On the other hand, the mental-health agency may have been achieving its own goals.

Rehabilitation agencies receive "points" for returning formerly disabled people to work. The number of clients that a rehabilitation agency can return to self-sufficiency is a statistic that a board understands. Difficult and long-term cases require more time than other cases. With severely limited staffs and facilities, rehabilitation workers are careful in choosing their clients. Other private and public agencies and institutions may not think that rehabilitation is doing its job, especially when those other agencies are unable to refer poor-risk clients to be helped. Each agency tries to limit the kinds of clients it accepts.

Frequently, social workers deal with clients who need legal aid. Social workers and lawyers are in the business of helping clients, but there are real differences in their areas of concern and their methods. Lawyers are concerned with their clients' legal rights—a relatively narrow perspective, both longitudinally and laterally. Social workers deal with the welfare of their clients in relation to society. Lawyers act as clients' representatives in court; social workers use a professional relationship with their clients in an effort to change the clients and their environment (Smith, 1972). Often, conflict results when a lawyer and a social worker try to work together to help a client. A social worker related this experience:

> One of the problems we had was a woman who absolutely, religiously believed that divorce was wrong and that she would be bedeviled if she divorced. She was told by Legal Aid that she could have help to get a divorce, but not a legal separation. She needed the legal separation to keep her husband from coming into the house and beating up her kids and her.

At this point, you might feel that referral of your clients is a lost cause. The time needed to go through the required steps in each agency is bad enough; when another agency is finally contacted, they may reject your request. If another agency accepts your request, you might not approve of their form of help. A family caseworker puts it this way:

> Legal Aid is swamped with cases, just like our agency is swamped with cases, and so is Mental Health. And so everybody's all swamped with cases, and everybody's pushing everything off on everyone else that they can. And what it really comes down to is the individual who's working with that family. What can that one individual caseworker do? Is that caseworker willing to invest the time and the energy and the hassling with Legal Aid or threatening

them by saying "This is an extreme case, and otherwise we'll have to remove the children from the home."

There is another means of making referrals and getting help for clients. Remember the nurse in the correctional institution whose clients needed medical treatment in hospitals? She discovered how to get around much of the bureaucratic red tape—she called cases "emergencies." A more common referral process involves the use of personal networks, or "who you know." One experienced helper puts it this way:

> If you know a specific person with whom you're kind of friends, and you say "Look, I really don't know what else to do, and I know that you can help with this situation. Is there any way you could free yourself up to do such and such?" If you have a friend, do something like this. I've got friends like that at Public Aid. I'll say "Hey, their caseworker is doing nothing. Who do I go to? What do I do?" And they'll tell me who to go to, and they will tell me the structure, when it's involved. But also they might even do it themselves. It's not like these things are just available. It's a lot of hard work, and it's partly hit and miss.

The development of a personal network of referral resources requires time. Established employees may be reluctant to share their network with you. This reluctance is due, in part, to the fact that these networks are built on reciprocity. I help you and your client; you help me and my client. Employees who share their networks with you may be creating an obligation to be fulfilled later.

Interorganizational Cooperation

Every human-service worker has a special "horror story" that illustrates the lack of cooperation and communication among service agencies. For example, when Aerospace Corporation spent 2.3 million tax dollars to design and equip ten police cars with the latest technology of crime fighting, nobody asked for input from police officers. As a result, the $10,000 minicomputer in the trunk tells the police officers in the car whether the siren is on or off (Mizelle, 1976), and a sensor indicates when the driver has his or her foot on the brake.

Less obvious but equally expensive examples are common. A little town where I once lived planned to build a Youth Center as a delinquency-prevention measure. Included in this structure would have been bath facilities, a gymnasium, and a game room. The town had two fully equipped structures that were not usually occupied during the times when the proposed Youth Center would have been busiest. These structures were public schools.

Since schools are found almost everywhere, and most of us have spent at least a decade or two in them, they are convenient and familiar examples of less-than-ideal helping institutions. "Too much school and not enough education" (Furst, 1975, p. 9) is one blanket condemnation. Furst (1975) and others, including Willower, claim that the primary purpose of schools seems to be to keep kids off the streets and out of the job market. Willower (1975) refers to schools as "A curious combination of the prison, the scout jamboree, and the situation comedy." Despite such criticisms, public schools hold the most potential for early problem identification and the subsequent delivery of solutions. "The times are ready for a new kind of pluralism in schooling; a pluralism which relates the schools with other institutions in carefully contrived and thoughtfully constructed ways" (Sizer, 1976, p. 34).

Carefully contrived and thoughtfully constructed ways won't guarantee help for a client from another agency. Cooperation among agencies isn't expected. Recently, I worked with a young man and his family. We were able to use an array of human services. A local juvenile police officer, a district probation officer, a detention home, a court psychologist, a family-service agency, a public defender, and two foster homes were involved. The case required patience and personal contacts. Despite all this, no magic happened. The man's family, and many who had contact with him, feel frustrated. The client does not yet resemble the community's model of a "good" person. He has not yet found his way. He is still exploring himself and the world around him. He will continue to change and grow in ways that are natural for him.

It is human to feel frustration when well-intended efforts don't seem to make a difference. Helping is hard work. When you know you have made a difference in a client's life, you feel fulfilled. When bureaucracy has gotten in the way of your help, you feel frustrated.

Summary

Very few agencies can provide all the services many clients need. You will probably work with a number of organizations; this experience may cause you to reevaluate your harsh judgment of your own organization. The formal referral process seldom works well. Agencies have differing goals and procedures. Often, many agencies compete for the same pot of tax money. Some agencies compete with one another for the same "turf."

Personal networks between the staff members of various agencies are more effective for referral than the formal systems. Such networks are developed over time and are based on reciprocity. Established employees may be reluctant to share their network with newcomers.

Discussion Questions

1. What are the general guidelines for deciding when and how to make referrals?
2. Describe your personal network on the job or in school. Whom do you know that can help you to get things done?

References

Epstein, I. Organizational careers, professionalism, and social worker radicalism. *Social Science Review*, June 1970, *44*(2), 127.

Furst, L. G. The educational fifth column: An expanded role for teachers. *Phi Delta Kappan*, September 1975, *57*(1), 8-10.

Goffman, E. *Asylums.* New York: Doubleday, 1961.

Lefton, M., & Rosengren, W. R. Organizations and clients: Lateral and longitudinal dimensions. *American Sociological Review*, 1966, *31*(6), 802-810.

Mizelle, W. R. LEAA space capsule on wheels ignores patrol car needs input by working police. *Police Times*, September 1976, *11*(7).

Sizer, T. R. Education and assimilation: A fresh plea for pluralism. *Phi Delta Kappan*, September 1976, *58*(1), 31-35.

Smith, A. D. The social worker in the legal aid setting: A study of interprofessional relationships. *The Social Service Review*, June 1972, *44*, 155-168.

Smith, L. M., & Geoffrey, W. *The complexities of an urban classroom: An analysis toward a general theory of teaching.* New York: Holt, Rinehart & Winston, 1968.

Willower, D. J. Some comments on inquiries on schools and pupil control. *Teachers' College Record*, 1975, *77*(2), 219-230.

7 Helplessness and Hope

Introduction

At times, your job as a human-service worker may seem to be part of a sham. You are unable to deal with real problems. You're busy using Band-Aids, instead of "miracle drugs"—treating symptoms, not causes. Others have shared this feeling of helplessness.

A child is referred to an agency for truancy. The immediate goal of the system is to return the child to school; however, the problem involves more than truancy:

> You're supposed to change something that's been going on for years and years and years. You're expected to do an impossible task. I remember a Black caseworker who was dealing with an extremely hostile White kid. This caseworker told me "I can't talk to this girl. She spits in my face. She's got to be in school. She just can't run in the streets, because somebody's going to get my ass if this kid isn't in school." I went down and talked to this girl. It was pretty obvious that she was in no condition to be in school. It was taking all her energy just to survive in her household. All the things school demands in terms of being able to put aside other problems and being able to know yourself, to accept yourself well enough to do the work you needed to do and not feeling so vulnerable to the other kids was beyond her. To cut it at all in school, even on a minimal level, was too much for this kid. I talked to her. I met her family and met her sister. I spent several hours with her and went back to the office and said "You know, this kid needs a lot of work, and she's not going to make

it in school right now," and the caseworker couldn't hear that. "But she's got to be in school; she's got to do something. She's either in school or she's got to work."

A nurse working in a public-health program had accepted another position. She felt that this would provide her an opportunity to tell the supervisor some things that would improve the services to their clients. She began her discussion in a very quiet tone of voice and told the supervisor that she had not come to criticize any employees, but rather to make some suggestions. She tells what happened:

> Before I left, I thought, well, this is my time when I can go tell the director of nurses about this stuff. Because we had this Medicheck [federally funded] program, and you were supposed to do certain things like get urinalysis and all this at certain times of the visit, and get the sickle cell, and get hemoglobin. They weren't making an attempt to get urinalysis, and I'd really get frustrated, because we wouldn't get our money from Medicheck. One thing that had to be on this Medicheck was just simple height and weight. We got out there [to the clinic] and there wasn't a scale, and there wasn't a tape measure. So we got none of the reimbursement. I was just floored at what she told me. She acted like I should just forget it.

A prison guard provides an example of how the rules, when they are applied in an institutional way, can do exactly the opposite of what they are intended to do (this is a follow-up to a case described in Chapter 1, in which an inmate threatened a guard's life):

> Later, he came to me one day and told me that he was due to go to parole board and wondered if I would write a letter for him to the board and maybe to the merit staff. I told him I would. He went to the parole board and got a year set [no parole hearing for another year]. He went back and created somewhat of a disturbance and today is in the segregation area, locked up because of his behavior again.

A worker in a mental hospital was responsible for a ward of ambulatory children who had not been outside for more than two weeks, even though the weather had been beautiful. He went to the supervisor in charge and offered to stay late after his shift was over to take the children out three afternoons per week for about an hour. The supervisor in this situation had a very real problem. She told him that she couldn't let him do that, because "We can't pay you over-time, and the hospital insurance would not cover you if any-thing happened to the children when you were outside with them." The hospital worker then went one step further up the administrative ladder. He puts it this way:

> I really started protesting about the kids not being taken out-side, and I wanted to work with them, so they started getting even with me by pulling me from one ward to another—making me dis-tribute tables to the hospital, that sort of thing, sending me to a ward with geriatrics where there's no real need for psychiatric aides, where I'd have to be changing bed sheets and stuff like that.

Unpredictable circumstances can improve client services. An institutional nurse took advantage of a change in adminis-trators to deliver health care to her clients, in spite of the rules and regulations of the organization:

> For the first six years that I worked there, it was literally im-possible to get a boy a pair of glasses. "We don't do that here. Our budget isn't set up for that." And about four years ago, we got a new superintendent and a new clinic director. I went down-town, talked to several optometrists, and got together with one of them. He gave us a fine, fair price on refracting the boys with visual problems. I went to the new clinic director and told him that six boys a month would be going, possibly eight at times, for refraction. And I just sort of included it as part of our format, and he said "Oh, you provide glasses here," and I said "We've always done it that way." So, for four years now the boys with visual problems have been getting glasses. I've never been called on it. If I ever am, I'll just say "Well, we've always done it that way."

The same nurse has successfully delivered service to her clients through a process described by her here. You might think that her methods are deceptive, dishonest, and unethical. This is your decision; in fact, it may be a decision that you will have to make. The nurse describes her methods this way:

> We get boys that are blind in one eye since birth, and nobody knows why. We get boys that have huge hernias. We have boys with torn knee cartilages and just a myriad of ailments. Well, our chief resource is _____ Hospital, which is also a state facil-ity, and, by reciprocal arrangements, we're supposed to be able to get services from them. It's much easier said than done. They want

you to write a letter and send a full history, and then they'll write back to you and let you know when the boy can have an appointment. When I first started to work there, it took upwards of four months sometimes to get an appointment for a boy. So I came to the conclusion that there had to be a better way. Now, when I get a boy who needs further care and needs it this week, not in three or four months, I do kind of a sneaky thing. I send them straight up to the hospital with a guard and a signed consent form that enables the hospital to treat them and send them straight to a patient screening clinic. This is where the people from the street walk in. I've gotten quite a few phone calls and a reprimand here and there from people at the hospital for doing that; but, that way, that kid is seen that day, and he has an appointment within the next five days to return for treatment. This saves a lot of time, and it saves a lot of stress and worry on the kids' part, and it probably doesn't really put the hospital off that much, because I've been doing it for years now.

If there's something that's not an emergency—doesn't need to be looked at right away—and they (our administrators) have no plans for transferring that boy immediately, then I go through legitimate channels.

A White female social worker assigned to a Black community by a state agency was having trouble relating to her clients, but then she found a "nonpolicy" means of relating to them:

We found that some of our clients were remarkably well-put-together people, and they could help other clients, so we had clients helping other clients and doing things with them. We had a lot of teenagers working for us as volunteers. Sometimes, a particular child of mine would be having problems, and I'd know that a certain one of the volunteer kids who was really in close contact with us in the office had had a similar problem and had worked it through, and I'd say "Would you talk to so-and-so?" And it built the volunteer's self-esteem to be able to do this, and yet also he got through to the child where I couldn't have.

The nurse and the social worker brought about change on their own; here, an English teacher describes a group effort to make change:

Nothing is so important to a teacher as his textbook. This Bible of the classroom, this expounder of all knowledge, is sacred as Holy Writ itself, and heaven help those pagans who fail to be guided by its pervasive knowledge. As might be expected, I had not fully realized this when I volunteered with sophomorish zeal to be on the committee to revise the textbook for freshman classes. After having experimented for one year with one freshman class without a textbook, I was to report to the group of teachers on how well the experiment went. After having completed this assignment, two of my English cohorts and I were to meet with the corresponding committee members from our sister school and make recommendations about texts. This we dutifully did. The attack on our recommendations came at the next department meeting.

Two veterans of 30 years' teaching had rallied their anti-new-textbooks associates and quickly made a frontal assault. They stormed the committee members with poignant questions, like "Why should this textbook be changed?" "What do these new books have that this book doesn't?" "Children are basically the same, so why change textbooks?" "A good story is timeless, isn't it?" Finally, they struck with their atomic question: "Have we voted on this change of textbook?"

They obviously had those recommending and favoring the adoption of a new textbook on the horns of a dilemma. For what true flag-carrying American could deny this privilege, this remnant of our democracy? The vote was taken, and the anti-new-textbook confederation had won. The committee members slid out of the room in a cloud of disgrace. My faith in the liberality of English teachers had been shaken. Where were the Deweys of yesteryear?

The war, however, was not over. Several teachers who were not present at the field of battle had not yet voted. When the absentee vote was counted, the conflict was stalemated: 11 *yes*, 11 *no*. Of course, the fortunes of war are fickle. The anti-new-textbook forces had had their moment in the sun. The returns from our sister school on the eastern front were nearly unanimous for the adoption of new freshman textbooks. And so, the battle of the books ended, and only a few remnants (an occasional snide comment, scornful glance, or uncomfortable silence) attested to the ferocity and intensity of this monumental war.

This description of a department's struggle to change one textbook illustrates the difficulty involved in bringing about change in an institution. Interdepartmental, intradepartmental, and administration/departmental problems are interwoven. Groups form. Traditionalists believe that those who want change are moving too swiftly, whereas enthusiasts assume that traditionalists will never change.

You may want to improve conditions and methods. You may want to effect changes. You may confront unresolved job conflicts. These unresolved conflicts can be frustrating and can produce a general feeling of tension. Supervisors will perceive this tension—some sooner than others. Your supervisors' reactions to your state depend on a variety of factors, including their mental health and their general attitudes and behavior toward employees. Their attitudes may range from "Let 'em bitch" to "I wonder what's wrong?" Their behavior may range from denial of problems to friendly counseling sessions and promotion. If you are a valued employee, if your tension hasn't become destructive, if an opening exists, and if your supervisor has read the research by Lieberman (1956) and Schein (1971), you may be promoted. Simply put, this research describes employees' change of attitude after promotion.

Burn Out: Its Treatment and Control

Job-related anxiety and unhappiness can affect not only your job but also the other areas of your life—if you allow it to do so. Your temper is quicker, your patience is shorter, your tolerance lower. Increased stress can lead to physical illness. When frustration reaches the point at which you can't stand it, you must do something. A carefully kept journal of the sort described in Chapter 3 can be of great help. By going back a few months and reading your entries, you may be able to understand how you developed the feelings you now experience. As you read what you wrote, look for significant events and people, as well as your reactions to them. Is there a pattern? What made you feel good? What made you feel bad? Can you change the way in which you spend your time on the job to get more of the "good" feelings and fewer of the "bad" feelings?

Your socialization coach may be someone within the system to whom you can go when you feel frustrated. When people who know you outside the job begin to ask "What's wrong?" it might be a good idea to tell them. Your spouse or roommate may assume that your unhappiness is being caused by them. By discussing the job situation with them, you let them know that it's not their fault, and you give yourself a chance to hear the words that describe your frustration. Your journal and your conversations may provide temporary relief. With some of the tension reduced, you may be able to think more clearly. Don't force yourself to choose between living with things as they are and quitting. When you're burned out, the choice may seem that simple, but it's more complex than that. For example, there are many ways of staying and many ways of quitting.

You can quit simply by not showing up, and soon you will be fired. You can go to work and mess up enough so that you get fired. You can sacrifice your job in a once-and-for-all showdown with the boss, in the hope that it will lead to improvements after you're gone. Let's assume that you have decided to stay and deal with burn out. The following examples may reflect your feelings. Perhaps the reactions of these new employees will be of help to you. (Some of these anecdotes were used earlier in a different context.)

> Then, the frustration of not being able to make progress became overwhelming. Everything I started became bogged down with paperwork, policies, and apathetic coworkers. It soon occurred to me that attempting to change the entire setup was unrealistic. So, I began to single out specific residents with specific problems and concentrated my efforts on them. By channeling my efforts on one resident at a time, I could actually see some positive results over a period of time. When one child learned to walk alone, or learned to feed himself, or was placed in a home setting, all the hassle was worthwhile.

A shift in focus from the larger organization and its problems to the individual client gave this employee temporary relief from the sense of being overwhelmed. This worked for her. For others, an emphasis on individual clients has been the primary cause of burn out.

> The first six months that I worked in this rural mental-health clinic, I felt so good when one of my people called me at home. It was kind of a high I got. I had really communicated caring and concern. They'd always apologize (for calling me at home), but I'd listen without showing any impatience. Once, even I called the supervising psychiatrist at home and got her to phone in a new prescription for this one client. It turned out that the client was really a drug-dependent person and had been using both our agencies and two local G.P.'s to supply drugs for the habit.
>
> Pretty soon, I liked the phone calls at home less and less. I began to distrust clients, and this distrust got communicated, I'm sure. My whole life was dependent on the success of my clients and the quality of my relationship with them.
>
> It has taken me more than two years to realize that a lot of my job is to help people change their values, beliefs, and behaviors. This process takes a long time. Deception is a way of life for a lot of my clients. It's not directed at me personally. People grow and change at different rates. It seems that some of them I can't help at all. Before I came to accept these things, I went so far as to get an unlisted [telephone] number. Now I just do the best I can,

and that's good. I have a job, but that job is not my life. My professional self is still related to my personal self, but not nearly so much. I feel a lot better this way.

A similar conclusion was drawn by a first-year English teacher who was having a lot of trouble getting her students interested in composition.

> I thought it might be interesting to try to start a newspaper. I brought this idea up to a couple of other teachers. "You have got to be kidding. You can't do that. Your class will get too loud. How are you going to teach gerunds and participles if you are going to print a newspaper?" Right away, I learned to keep my mouth closed and to go ahead and do something if I wanted to do it, without telling anybody.
>
> After what I've been through, I come to the conclusion that you have to find the strength within yourself to survive these things. You've got to come to grips with them and decide what's important to you and for whom you are working. I was terrified, depressed, and disillusioned for the first year, and am still disillusioned now. At least I know what's real, and I know I have made my choice. All I have to do is carry through. As long as you're happy with yourself, you can tolerate what's around and above you.

The attitudes of your coworkers may support your feelings of despair and frustration. Established employees who come across as cruel, indifferent, and incompetent may have been burned out as a result of a series of events. They seem not to care. Perhaps they were dedicated staff members and helpful supervisors; now they passively accept what has become a norm for them. They may be resigned to accepting things as they are. Acceptance of things as they are doesn't have to mean acceptance of things as unchanging. The next section provides some guidelines for change.

So Now You Want to Change the Organization

What can you as an individual do, and how should you go about attempting to change those practices and policies that, in your judgment, need to be altered? There is a wide range of positions that can be taken. One position addresses the basic institutions themselves. Adherents of this position seek to rearrange the structure and roots of power. They would free the institutions from what they see as outworn bureaucratic strictures, political associations, and social-class influences. For example, they would redistribute income, rather than provide specialized government programs for housing, health, and education.

At the other extreme, the concept of change does not address institutions; instead, it focuses on individuals in an effort to help them to cope. Simply put, the focus is on the preparation of each individual to effectively deal with the bureaucratic institutions that are designed to deliver services. Such a position focuses the development of skills and competencies that are needed to overcome the bureaucratic institution's shortcomings. Adherents of this position hold that those of us who develop and practice these skills at the highest level will be the most successful members of our society.

These positions regarding institutional change could place every human-service practitioner in a dilemma—to choose one or the other. Even if one assumes that these two alternatives— either revolutionizing the institutional structures or focusing on the development of individuals—are of equal value, it gives little hope to the practitioner. The hard facts of the matter are that there are no equal alternatives. Our society is not on the brink of a revolution; it seems that a total and systematic forward-looking change is not going to occur in the near future. If such a revolution were to occur, it would undoubtedly be more effectively carried out by the masses of youthful nonprofessionals rather than by professional human-service practitioners.

For us, there is another option—a middle level of social change and direct practice that focuses on both the individual and the institution. I suggest this middle position for those of you who are attempting to survive as well as service your client populations. I believe that the practitioner must recognize basic social problems as well as the criticisms appropriately made about the direct practice of help giving. Action through practice to deal with institutional dysfunction while improving service to clients is the challenge we all face. This challenge will test your ability to maintain a balance between your technical competence, your psychological health, and your ability to "step away" and see the larger picture.

Your decision to be a human-service worker implies an acceptance of your clients' immediate problems and their concern with their environments. You have been trained to know about the strains—social, economic, physiological, and psychological—with which clients must cope. The awareness of these realities must be tempered by a continued awareness of the environment in which the bureaucracy places you.

Ready or not, you are expected to be a help giver and a bureaucrat. To state the issue directly, you have technical competencies and skills, but you are probably unprepared for organizational life. You need bureaucratic skills in order to capitalize on the possibility for organizational change as well as to neutralize stresses and strains that will be placed on you. An understanding of the bureaucratic process will provide an opportunity for self-direction. The acquisition of bureaucratic skills may lead to greater satisfaction on the job as well as higher levels of professional accomplishment.

It is unproductive to think of bureaucracy as "bad"—as something to be overcome. Bureaucracy can be understood as a complex environment in which purposes are pursued. Often, these purposes are blurred, as each member of the bureaucracy privately pursues goals that are most important to him or her. The bureaucratic environment can be so confusing to the newcomer that he or she simply becomes debilitated. As you look at the established staff in your group, you see individuals who have followed the path of least resistance. The help-giving bureaucrat who is satisfied with the status quo is not uncommon. For those who are not satisfied—those who hold visions of what their organizations might be—discretion and research are vital resources.

First, you should research your relationship with your supervisor, specifically focusing on the content of your job as it is viewed by that supervisor. Your supervisor will have some conception of the job that you are expected to perform. Although the specifications of your job may be partly determined by organizational rules derived from a statutory base, they were most likely established by one or more previous job holders—one of whom may have been your supervisor. Once you are clearly aware of the supervisor's view of your job, you can begin to estimate where he or she might be in terms of anticipating the kinds of arguments that will be presented to you during any future disagreements.

Many opportunities to initiate progress are open only to those who work within the system. By listening and looking, you will gain opportunities to help move your organization in one direction rather than another. All organizations change.

Sometimes organizations change because they want to, but more basically, they do so because they cannot avoid it. For any given bureaucrat, the *kind* of changes he or she wants may not have occurred; or they may occur too slowly; or the individual may feel that she or he plays no part in the process; or for many reasons, the individual may be discouraged about it or oblivious to it. But none of this alters the fact that the forces and pressures that produce change are at play in organizations at least as powerfully and persistently as are those that promote stability. A crude but fair test of this proposition is the difficulty that anyone would have in identifying even a single organization that is today precisely as it was even a year or two ago. No such organization exists or ever will. The conventional wisdom on the subject, which implies that bureaucracy, unlike everything else in this world, has somehow immunized itself against change, is simply incorrect.

Organizational change is a continuous process rather than a sporadic event; everthing [sic] affects everything. Things are always happening that make it easier to press certain initiatives and harder to press others: a staff member quits, and so some clique or alliance is strengthened or weakened; the organization moves to another building with a different layout of office space, so the director casually observes one unit more often and another less often while heading for lunch each day; the budget is reduced, held the same, or enlarged, inducing some to throw up their hands in disgust and others to compete more aggressively for everything in sight; one kind of client problem appears less frequently and another more frequently. Each of these events upsets the equilibrium of the system to some degree, making it more internally fluid than it was before. The bureaucrat who is sensitive to these things and can think a few moves ahead is the one who is most likely to see that some greater or lesser nuance in the organization's evolution occurs because he or she willed it. Though change is the most continuous organizational process, the responsibility to bring it about is part of no individual job description [Baer & Federico, 1978].[1]

Effective change comes neither in large chunks nor as a result of showdowns and other dramatic occurrences. Rather, it is an almost daily process of small adjustments, each of which makes succeeding adjustments more or less likely to occur. The combination of these changes shapes the organization. With skill, careful planning, and good research, effective change will come in small quiet increments and will be produced through persistent action based on careful observation of your organization.

Unless your research tells you otherwise, your supervisor is probably the first one you should talk to if you want to make any changes in the way things are done. Before you

[1] Reprinted with permission from *Educating the Baccalaureate Social Worker*, Volume 1, Copyright 1978, Ballinger Publishing Company.

make the approach, consider this: you must be far enough into your present job to be fully socialized, yet far enough away from your next job to be fully involved in your present position. If you are too close to your next job, you may be seen as a "lame duck." Now, if you've decided to go ahead, lay out the problems you have seen and ask for advice and counsel. This will make your supervisor feel helpful; moreover, your supervisor may have a good idea regarding the problems you've come to discuss.

It is difficult to make real changes in an organization. Although there are many theories regarding organizational change, no workable theory has yet emerged. In *Managing Organizational Innovations*, O'Connell (1968) provides a conceptual framework that serious readers may find helpful in avoiding some mistakes as they try to change organizations. Don't expect any pat answers in any of the literature. Three experts from Canada studied the process of high-level decision making in organizations and concluded that not enough is known to provide even an elementary understanding of how organizations function (Mintzberg & Théorêt, 1976).

Seven widely recognized authorities in educational administration (Charters, Everhart, Jones, Packard, Pellegrin, Reynolds, & Wacaster, 1973, p. 105) documented the lack of success in implementing planned change in public schools and came to two conclusions: (1) the chances of making changes are small, and (2) the knowledge that explains how to make changes, if such knowledge exists, is a well-guarded secret.

DiNunzio, Willower, and Lynch (1976), three experts in administration, carefully document the reasons for the relative failure of a change attempt. They conclude that "Much of what occurred could be explained by the nature of school social structure." Often, attempts to effect changes in organizations fail because the attempts are sucked into the system. Social-welfare agencies and health-care agencies try to coordinate services for multiproblem families through team approaches, between-agency case conferences, and new legislation. Such attempts to provide better service to clients usually result in the hiring of additional people, which creates additional professional jobs and another layer of bureaucracy (Fainstein & Fainstein, 1972).

At times, attempted changes are treated as experiments or demonstrations. The special status of "innovation" threatens the life of the attempted change. First, the new program is given its own special budget. Second, the originators are pleased when the boss proudly points the program out to visiting dignitaries and mentions it in the annual report; however, once the program has lost its public-relations value, the special budget on which it has become dependent may well disappear.

Often, organizational change attempts, or innovative programs, are isolated from the larger system. "It and the rest of the system become rigid separately, in defense against one another" (Lynton, 1969, p. 400). The isolation produces a win-or-lose situation—a battle between the "new" and the "old." The old "has a crust of traditional practices which nothing short of dynamite can remove" (Levy & Herzog, 1971, p. 199). Usually, the "old" controls a loyal army.

Levy and Herzog described a program change that was deliberately set up parallel to, but isolated from, an existing program. The new program had a special budget. Due to its budget and its isolation, the new program's chances of survival were almost nonexistent.

Now for some hope. Organizations *do* change. Why do they change? More important to you, how can they be changed? The most honest answer to these questions is that nobody really knows, but we have begun to find some answers. Some of the major conditions for promoting and sustaining change, or organizational innovations, are discussed in the next section.

Some Conditions That May Make Your Change Efforts Successful

First, ask your immediate supervisor for help. The answer to your request may indicate how he or she would react to your direct suggestions. In the process of giving you help, your supervisor may think of the idea that you had. There are few things more powerful than a boss with an idea that he or she thinks may work. One staff member put it this way: "I'd kept the idea up in the minds of the administrators and all of a sudden they thought it was a great idea." In other words, "those who had power, sanctions, and communication linkages and boundary roles appeared to be important in the adoption of innovations" (Baldridge & Burnham, 1975, p. 175). This means that those who control resources, rewards, punishments, and contacts are more likely to bring about change than those who don't have such control.

Although you may feel better after you've complained to the boss about a particular problem, complaining won't solve the problem, and it probably won't help the boss to feel better. Before you present a problem to your supervisor, draw up a list of possible solutions. You should order your solutions, beginning with the best one and ending with the one that you like the least.

There may be times when you feel that you need to go around rules and regulations—to skip some links in the chain of command. Devito (1974), who is a psychiatrist turned hospital administrator, says that such behavior is probably a symptom of organizational anxiety. As an administrator, he would react in a rather neutral way if you went directly to him with a suggestion or a complaint. At least he would not punish you for making an appointment. Not all administrators feel this way. When you can't get what you think you ought to have from your immediate superiors, you need to ask yourself this question: "Will going around them to get what I want be worth the price I may have to pay?" Even if you win this time and get what you want, what about tomorrow?

If you decide to go around your immediate superiors, tell them that you are going to see their boss. (If you ask for their permission, they may refuse.) When you have chosen to tell your supervisors that you're going to see the boss, don't expect the next person up the line to support you or to be pleased to see you. Your visit indicates that something is amiss. Waves may be coming. The status quo is being threatened. If your immediate supervisor insists on going with you to see the boss, the boss probably won't support your position in your supervisor's presence; organizational morale depends on the boss's support of your supervisor. If the big boss believes that you are right, your supervisor may get chewed out after you leave. Even if your immediate supervisor is not present when you talk to the boss, it is very likely that the boss has already been briefed in advance on the issue and been presented with the arguments you have used unsuccessfully with your supervisor. Therefore, you should be prepared to present new and stronger arguments. Continued appeal to higher authority usually follows a particular process—your arguments are conveyed to the next in command before you arrive. It can be a tough road. Be careful. Gather as much information as possible about the people and the issues involved.

An experienced security officer in an institution for delinquents has this advice: "If you feel you've got to do it, make sure what you're trying to do is important enough. You have to use good judgment and common sense when you decide to buck the system." You should remember that: (1) all of the details need to be worked out ahead of time; (2) if you don't follow up every detail, your efforts are likely to fail; (3) many of the people with whom you will deal mean well but don't really know what they are doing, or why; and (4) you probably haven't thought of the best answer, so keep asking yourself the question.

When you go to see your supervisor, or when your supervisor comes to you, don't cover too much ground. Don't try to cure the ills of the world with one program change. (You will have time to reform the CIA next year!) Simply put, don't bring up irrelevant issues. Keep your personal beliefs to yourself. Deal only with issues that are directly related to the change that you want to discuss. International politics and religious beliefs probably don't have anything to do with it.

One alternative to the direct approach is the "everything is ready to go" approach. You have thought out all of the possible problems that will be created by the change you want to make. You have at least one solution for each of the problems. The budget will not be hurt. Other staff members' turf has been protected or negotiated. Other agencies and organizations have informally agreed to your proposal. The professional literature, such as newsletters, journals, and recent books, indicate that your proposed change is a good idea. The change will help the clients. The risk is small. The change will be a feather in the boss's cap. This strategy involves time and the help of other people. The majority of these other people will mean well and intend to keep their commitment to you when the chips are down, but some may not. It is a good idea to be "two deep." Each necessary element in your plan should have at least one alternative, in case somebody backs out or something goes wrong. The character Chicken George in the television production *Roots* demonstrated this strategy. Planning, coordination, and constant follow-up are key factors in this approach to change. Putting together such a package will require time beyond your normal working hours. The wrapping on this ready-to-go package is the potential benefit to the image of your organization and its leaders.

An example of an "everything is ready to go" program is provided by the vocational-training program developed by a youth supervisor in a correctional institution. He modified the strategy by using a stepwise approach. The key elements in his package included the following: no financial cost, negotiated turf, a potentially therapeutic program for clients, more efficient utilization of staff skills, an agreement with major unions, tax-deductible contributions from community businesses, and a lot of patience.

One of the things that I felt was badly needed out there at the institution was a program that a kid could get into that would do him some good when he got back out on the street. A lot of kids liked mechanical work—things they could do with their hands. They didn't need a lot of books, because a lot of those kids couldn't read. They can't use figures too well.

I felt that small engine mechanical repair work must be a place to begin. I was told that it couldn't be done, because we didn't have the equipment, money to buy the equipment, or a qualified teacher. So it was just kind of sloughed off.

Well, I still felt that the program was worthwhile. I believed in it, so I kept at it—still getting the same answers, until one day I got a little disgusted with the whole thing, and I decided that I would get equipment someplace, and I would teach it myself. I had been an auto mechanic for about 20 years, so I went downtown to [a retail chain store] and I talked to the manager. I explained to him what I had in mind and that we needed tools to be able to do the work. He told me he would check it out with his superiors and let me know in a couple of weeks.

Two weeks went by and, sure enough, they came out with a nice set of tools for us. That was a big step, and then they also threw in five or six small engines. So I went back to the institution with it and said "Now I've got the tools, I have the engines to work on. Now let's see if we can't get this set up." They came back with "Well, we don't have any place to put it, no room to accommodate that kind of job program."

At that time, we had one wing in our building that we didn't operate anymore, and there were 16 rooms back in the wing. They were small rooms, but I felt that we could take and knock a wall out between two rooms and make one workshop out of it. I went up and asked the superintendent about it. He said "Well, can you get the boys to do it?" I said "They would jump at the chance to try to knock a jail down." So he said "Well, you'll have to check with the union on it." And, of course, the union said that we couldn't do it, because there would probably be supervisors or somebody around there other than the boys that would be doing the work. We had a little hassle over that, but they finally agreed that I could use boys to knock the walls down in the two rooms where I wanted to make a workshop. The boys were enthusiastic. They made a work bench, painted it, painted the cabinets, and we moved in with our tools and the cabinets. We were able to have five boys in the morning class.

Now I felt that the workshops could be expanded. We could have a wood shop. I had listened to the boys and heard a lot of boys say that they'd like to do a little wood work, and we set up a wood shop.

I had heard where manufacturers farmed out work from the company to different places to have work done. I went to a company in [a small town] and talked to the president, and he had room on an assembly line to put radar ranges together. I went back to the institution and presented the idea to the superintendent. We had boys assigned from one of the programs on an outside job which had been a failure. I was informed by the superintendent that it was against state law. It was against the law to bring work in and have boys work on it. It would be kind of like a . . . considered a sweat shop thing, I suppose. But he did call the state capitol and ask about it, and it kind of went into limbo, so I kept toying around with the idea.

I kept the idea up in their minds and up in front. Eventually, they decided that the programs were a good idea. Some of our boys now get skills, earn a salary, and have a good reason to read and work with numbers.

In one sense, the following strategy is a variation of the "everything is ready to go" approach. The big difference is that, in using this approach, you use the power of the structure in order to affect the bureaucracy. If you want to play high stakes, this is a long shot that works best in big, state-controlled organizations. In other words, "Large complex organizations with a heterogeneous environment are more likely to adopt innovations than a small, simple organization with a relatively stable, homogeneous environment" (Baldridge & Burnham, 1975, p. 175).

After you have completed the checklist of financial costs, potential problems and corresponding solutions, other staff and agency turf, improved service to clients, and an estimate of the board's response, two additional major items must be considered before you take this approach. First, be sure that your plans do not interfere with any private profit being made by your superiors. Second, you must be able to afford clothing, food, and shelter (in case your plans don't work). This approach is similar to the "everything is ready to go" strategy, except that it involves an additional step: you need to obtain the support of the state director, the government, or the council—that is, the really big boss. (At times, the really big boss is money. A federal grant can be the equivalent of the big boss's approval.)

How can you manage to see the really big boss? Most state directors' offices are in the state capitol. Whatever you do, *don't* make an appointment. If you do, an administrative aide will want to know the nature of your visit in advance; this could involve your lower-level bosses. At this point, you do not want them to be involved. Find out when the state director is in, and go to his office. Do this on your own time. Just walk in. Tell the receptionist that you have an idea that will either improve the service to clients or reduce the agency's budget, but that you need the director's advice and counsel. Indicate that you will wait, that it will take only a few minutes, and that you would be happy to see the director between scheduled appointments. At this point, you may think that this strategy won't work. ("They'll never let me in!") Maybe you are right. That's one of the chances you have to take.

State directors can easily become isolated from what is going on at the grassroots level. They have most likely been away from the action for a long time. At one time, they may have been professional helpers. Within the limits of professional ethics, you are asking them to participate with another professional in formulating organizational goals (Wade, 1967). In order to participate effectively, they need to know what is going on at the grassroots level. This creates a conflict, because they don't know what's really going on, and they don't know how to find out. Your visit represents a chance for them to get out with the real world of their organizations without ever leaving their offices. They see your visit as an opportunity to visit the troops without actually going into the field.

When you are introduced to state directors, the weather (and other light topics) will be discussed, as they are in any uncomfortable social situation. Once you've begun to feel comfortable, get right to the point. Have your story prepared. Practice in the presence of some intelligent listeners. Don't memorize, but have a key-word outline in your head. Your entire pitch shouldn't require more than three minutes. Of course, you have to allow the directors to interrupt with questions. Answer them straightforwardly, and go on to the next part of your outline. Remember, don't discuss unrelated personal beliefs that may be controversial. Listen closely to any sign of interest. Be sensitive to nonverbal messages that indicate that it's time for you to leave: if the director looks away from you, gazes at papers on the desk, or stands up, your time is up. The director shouldn't have to open the door to the office in order to indicate that it's time for you to go.

When you go home and tell your local boss that the state director thinks you have a good idea, all hell will break loose. Don't try to stop it. When your immediate supervisor calms down, it might help if you say that you told the state director that only under the guidance of a manager like yours could your proposal be carried out. Allow your superiors to have a genuine role in the planning and control of the new program as soon as possible. If they are to be committed to the program, they must feel that at least a part of the change is their idea. Also, since your superiors most likely have been around the organization longer than you have, they will be able to see problems that you have not seen, find solutions that you didn't think of, and open local doors more easily than you can. If you get this far, good luck, careful planning, and constant follow-up are the keys.

One consequence of this change strategy is that some staff members at your level may be threatened and jealous: threatened, because they aren't sure what the change will do to them and their jobs; jealous, because they wish that they had the nerve to do what you have done. Four outcomes of this strategy are described in the following paragraphs.

A street-therapy program is operating under the sponsorship of a state mental-health clinic servicing a severely depressed urban area. Through the program, both professional and paraprofessional mental-health workers provide client services in homes rather than having all of the clients come to a clinic. At the time the program was initiated, it was a novel idea. All the steps listed earlier were a part of the planning of this program. The support of the state director was secured by the social worker in a manner very similar to the one described here. The local mental-health clinic and its local director have received state-wide recognition and considerable support and cooperation from other help-giving agencies in the community.

Another successful application of this change strategy resulted in a new treatment program for institutionalized delinquents in direct helping roles with geriatric mental patients in a state hospital. The Associated Press and CBS devoted feature stories and television programming to the dramatic results of this program. The administrations of the institution for the delinquents and the state mental hospital received state-wide awards for the program. This program change was initiated through a combination of federal grant money and visits to the state director's offices.

The third example of this strategy involves the development of a halfway house for adult criminal offenders. In this case, the "state director" was a combination of a state supreme court judge, the state bar association, and an officer of a police chiefs' association, each of whom expressed approval to their local counterparts.

A program that was initiated by a prison psychologist who had carefully planned and even operated a small-scale drug-treatment program for inmates had negative results. The psychologist had methodically developed all of the necessary support at the local level and had gotten the state director's blessing. The program had been in operation for two months when the psychologist was invited to participate in a professional conference. Upon checking into his hotel room, he saw that there were empty whiskey bottles and lipstick-covered cigarette butts in the trash can and assumed that the room had not been cleaned. Eventually, he suspected that perhaps this was not the case, because the rest of the room seemed to be in good order. Having worked with inmates for some time, he had become wise to the ways of the street. He began a more methodical search of the room and discovered a small bag of marijuana taped to the back of the toilet tank. He removed the bag of marijuana, took it down to the desk clerk, and asked that his room be changed. Within ten minutes, three squad cars of the local police arrived at the hotel to search the room that the psychologist had originally been given. It turned out that he had been set up because his drug-treatment program was interfering with a lieutenant and three guards who had been selling illicit drugs to inmates.

Administrative approval—support from your boss in dealing with the initial reactions of coworkers—gives you a good start in changing what you set out to change. But it's only a start. The good feelings of accomplishment and reward are luxuries to be enjoyed. Now the real work begins. To make the change work—to really help clients—could be a lifelong task. The hardest part is to get the ball rolling, especially when you have been pushing uphill. The ball will stop, and may even roll back, if you stop pushing. The upgrade is long, so don't use all your energy at the bottom. A steady flow of problems will come your way. The more problems you have predicted, the more ready you will be to deal with them— they may not become crises. For example, in the program mentioned earlier, (Russo, 1974) in which delinquents worked in a mental hospital, it was predicted that contraband would be brought into the delinquents' treatment center from the hospital and that sexual contacts would be made between the delinquent boys and the female patients and staff at the hospital. Tentative means of dealing with these kinds of problems were worked out in advance. Incidents of these types occurred and were handled with little fuss. If the incidents had not been predicted and alternative solutions hadn't been worked out, the new program might have been stopped by the alleged rape of a hospital staff member by one of the boys. The best protection against the development of crises is preplanning, followed by open communication between the staff and administration. Your organization's policies and traditions may dictate the form of this communication; but, whatever the form, it should be frequent and open. It is especially important to give those who are against the changes every chance to explain their points of view. If they are given a chance to disagree and be heard, they may change their minds.

Let's review some of the conditions that may make your attempt at change successful. Those who control resources, rewards, punishments, and contacts are more likely to effect change than those who lack such power. Can you identify these characteristics in the examples listed in the past few pages? What were the resources—money, ideas, or something else? What were the rewards and punishments, and for whom were they intended? Who were the contacts? Did these examples contain all the characteristics needed for successful change?

If your clients are concerned, they may be of some help in keeping the change process going. Remember to respect the delicate position of the clients. When it is used carefully, pressure can be effective. "The presence of militant client demands makes it rational, in terms of bureaucratic survival, to do something rather than nothing" (Fainstein & Fainstein, 1972, p. 519). The use of client demands to help bring about a change needs to be included in the detailed planning and the detailed follow-up. To repeat an earlier caution, your clients may mean well, but they probably won't know quite what they are doing or why they are doing it. They will need leadership.

Division, tension, and conflict within an organization will help to initiate change. Despite careful recruitment and intensive socialization pressures, some dissenters get into the ranks. Conflicting organizational goals are common. This problem is clearly illustrated in prisons, where rehabilitation and custodial goals coexist (Presthus, 1960). Reduced budgets and pressure for greater efficiency produce tension in almost all organizations.

Conflict, Competition, and Cooperation

As we saw earlier, most of us view *conflict* as a bad word; however, conflict also can be viewed as the engine that helps start change and the engine that keeps it moving.

Survival requires change. Organizational norms of apathy and "harmony at all costs" allow poor decisions to go unquestioned. Robbins (1974, p. 9) claims that "more organizations are dying from complacency and apathy than are dying from an overabundance of conflict." The value of conflict in group decision making was clearly demonstrated by Boulding (Kahn & Boulding, 1964, p. 147) when, as an experiment, she purposely placed "deviants" in some groups who were told to solve a problem. Other groups did not have a person who challenged and questioned the popular, or majority, position. In every case, the groups in which the deviants were placed came up with richer and more elegant solutions. But watch out! When each of Boulding's groups was asked to oust one member, every group that contained a deviant member chose to drop that member.

Here, and in earlier chapters, I have come across as being in favor of conflict; however, I do not advocate all kinds and intensities of conflict. Some conflict is functional; it supports goals and improves performance. On the other hand, conflict can be dysfunctional. The distinction between these two types of conflict isn't always clear. Those who value the status quo will view conflict differently than those who want change. For those who are seriously interested in this topic, *Managing Organizational Conflict* (Robbins, 1974) is an excellent source of information.

Compared to *conflict*, the word *competition* is much more "American." The free enterprise system is intended to be guided by competition. Competition for scarce resources can lead to conflict. In this kind of a situation, one party in the competition gains at the expense of the other. This kind of competition leads to conflict. Competition between departments, wards, cell blocks, or classes for the highest percentage of blood donors will not likely cause conflict. The point is that, although competition and conflict are two distinct concepts, they are sometimes related.

Many managers and supervisors believe that cooperation is the opposite of conflict. These people believe that, if they can stifle conflict, cooperation will result. It isn't so—especially in large bureaucratic organizations.

Large formal structures produce both isolation and segregation. The organizational rewards available to key staff members come from the part of the organization for which you work, not the department with whom you cooperate. You and your clients will find some people who cooperate for reasons that have little to do with organizational reward. Use that cooperation with the knowledge that no one is being paid for it.

Remember, You're a Guest

If you are an intern, student teacher, or trainee, you shouldn't try to make any real changes in the organization in which you are receiving your training. You are there to see what the place is really like, not to change it. The host organization and your school have carefully agreed to the terms of your apprenticeship. If you violate those terms, your actions could cost students coming after you the opportunity of having a work experience. If the experience is more false than real, tell your department chairperson or the dean; do not try to change the host organization while you are a student.

Clinical experiences for student teachers and nurses in college-degree programs usually are arranged in a local school and hospital. Students' time and allegiance are shared by the teachers and the hospital supervisors. The student is subjected to the sometimes contradictory pronouncements and justifications of each group. The students can't remain neutral, because, while they're in school, the teaching faculty controls their destiny and their loyalty. Since the clinical experiences are brief in every specialty area, the student nurse does not have time or interest to develop loyalties to the school or to the hospital; however, after graduation, conflict begins.

As a part of the university program, student teachers must perform for a university supervisor. And, as a part of the host school, they must perform to meet the standards of the cooperating teacher. Obviously, then, much of the value of student teaching is determined by the luck of the draw—the people to whom the student teachers are assigned by the university and the host school. The idea is to satisfy both the university supervisor and the cooperating teacher. The student teachers' position is usually compounded by a number of other things. For instance, student teachers are frequently placed in communities in which they have few friends. Moreover, they find it difficult to find apartments that are within a student's budget. At the host school, student teachers are treated with an abrupt kindness. Having been introduced to a few teachers, isolated student teachers seek them out during lunch periods and free hours. While other teachers are busy grading papers or talking about students they have had, student teachers feign interest or pretend to be engrossed in books. As a result, many student teachers feel comfortable only in the company of cooperating teachers and a few other colleagues, usually in the same age bracket. In fact, student teachers in secondary schools report that the students usually make them feel more comfortable than the faculty members do.

Your administrative superiors are neither idiots nor geniuses. They are people who feel good when they are respected, needed, and genuinely complimented. They feel bad when they are sick, threatened, and put down. When they are approached as humans for advice and counsel or with well-conceived and carefully planned suggestions, many administrators will listen carefully, ask clarifying questions, and be generally supportive of staff members who want to improve services. It is a pleasure to have such an administrative superior.

When you try to make changes, remember that every organization is unique to some degree. Each organization has its own unique history, goals, and position in the larger social structure. Despite this fact, some responses to change are common to all organizations. For example, as Gamsen (1968, p. 146) has pointed out, "When an organization has exhausted its supply of social controls, either because it has few available or because the attempted social controls were ineffective, organizational modification should occur."

Summary

At one point, your job as a human-service worker may seem like part of a sham. You are confronted by one agency, under bureaucrats, with liberty and service for some. You don't deal with real problems. You're busy using Band-Aids instead of miracle drugs—treating symptoms, not causes. You may want to make changes. First, you need to accept things as they are. (Accepting doesn't mean becoming resigned to the status quo.)

A series of case examples in this chapter illustrates some of the conditions that may make your change efforts successful. Conflict, competition, and cooperation are important elements in the dynamics of change and survival. More important is the way in which you deal with the tension and anxiety that results from frustration.

Discussion Questions

1. In addition to talking to a friend and reading your personal journal, list some socially acceptable means of reducing job tension.
2. What would be the costs to you for going to the director (or dean) to try to make a change in the way things are done by your supervisor (or teacher)? What effect would your behavior have on your continuing relationship with your supervisor (or teacher)?
3. What is the relationship between your change (or proposed change) and the rest of the system? How are they linked? Can you change one part of a system without affecting the entire system?
4. What power do you have as a staff person or student?

References

Baer, B. L., & Federico, R. *Educating the baccalaureate social worker.* Cambridge, Mass.: Ballinger Publishing Company, 1978.

Baldridge, J. V., & Burnham, R. A. Organizational innovation: Individual, organizational and environmental impacts. *Administrative Science Quarterly*, Summer 1975, *20*.

Charters, W. W., Jr., Everhart, R. B., Jones, J. E., Packard, J. S., Pellegrin, R. J., Reynolds, L. J., & Wacaster, C. T. *The process of planned change in the school's instructional organization.* CASEA Monograph No. 25, University of Oregon, Eugene, 1973.

Devito, R. A. The supervisory bypass: A symptom of organizational anxiety. *Hospital and Community Psychiatry*, 1974, *25*(11).

DiNunzio, J., Willower, D. I., & Lynch, F. Some consequences of a sponsored innovation in an elementary school. *Journal of Educational Administration*, October 1976, *14*(2), 187-191.

Fainstein, N., & Fainstein, S. Innovation in urban bureaucracies. *American Behavioral Scientist*, March 1972, *15*(4).

Gamsen, Z. F. Organizational responses to members. *The Sociological Quarterly*, Spring 1968.

Kahn, R. L., & Boulding, E. *Power and conflict in organizations.* New York: Basic Books, 1964.

Levy, L., & Herzog, A. N. The birth and demise of a planning unit in a state mental health department. *Community Mental Health,* September 1971, 7(3).

Lieberman, S. The effects of changes in roles on the attitude of role occupants. *Human Relations,* 1956, 9, 385-402.

Lynton, R. P. Linking an innovation subsystem into the system. *Administrative Science Quarterly,* September 1969, 14(3).

Meyer, C. H. *Social work practice* (2nd Ed.). New York: Free Press, 1976.

Mintzberg, H. D. R., & Théorêt, A. The structure of "unstructured" decision process. *Administrative Science Quarterly,* June 1976, 21.

O'Connell, J. *Managing organizational innovations.* Homewood, Ill.: R. D. Irwin, Inc., 1968.

Presthus, R. V. Authority in organizations. *Public Administration Review,* Spring 1960, 20.

Robbins, S. P. *Managing organizational conflict: A new traditional approach.* Englewood Cliffs, N. J.: Prentice-Hall, 1974.

Russo, J. R. Mutually therapeutic interaction between mental patients and delinquents. *Hospital and Community Psychiatry,* August 1974, 25(8).

Schein, E. H. The individual, the organization, and the career: A conceptual scheme. *Journal of Applied Behavioral Science,* 1971, 7, 401-426.

Wade, L. L. Professionals in organizations: A neoteric model. *Human Organization,* Spring and Summer 1967, 26(1,2).

8

Odds and Ends from the Present and a Look at the Future

Committees

Like almost everything else in bureaucratic organizations, committees can be ranked in order of importance. Committees that deal with organizational structure have the highest bureaucratic status, and those that deal with client welfare have the lowest status; the others fall somewhere between these two. Promotion, salary, and hiring committees are near the top. Those dealing with routine organizational maintenance, such as the revision of paper forms or the planning for the staff party, are near the bottom. Somewhere in the middle are task forces, which administrators call committees, if they think they might be important. For a more detailed and delightfully funny description of committee hierarchy, read Kolstoe's *College Professoring* (1975).

As a staff member, you will have an opportunity to be appointed or elected to various committees. If you are a good committee member, the chance for more service to the organization will follow quickly. If you are really good, you could become a committee chairperson. Good committee members attend, are attentive, speak a little, and volunteer to help write the committee report. Look at your organization's committee structure, how it operates, what it accomplishes, and where you want to participate—if at all.

Consultants

Almost all organizations use consultants. These are people who are brought in to advise on specific areas or problems. Usually, they're paid by the day—their pay is called an *honorarium*. Consultants are chosen because they are well-known in a particular field, have important contacts, believe what the boss believes, or, more often, because they used your boss as a consultant last year. For whatever reason they are chosen, and regardless of how much they are paid, you will see little of them and be only temporarily (if at all) influenced by them or their report. Prior to their arrival, you will be told to be honest in answering their questions. It is not unusual for a consultant to come in before your organization is due to be accredited, inspected, or evaluated. A good report from a consultant can be used to impress outside evaluators.

Accrediting, Inspecting, and Evaluating
Human-Service Organizations

On a regular basis, your organization will be examined by a state, regional, or national body to see that it meets some minimum standards. You will know when one of these visits is about to occur. The organization's paper work will be put in order. You will be asked to look over your own personnel file to see that all of your latest training, honors, publications, and other achievements have been listed. Hospital staffs will scramble to keep their nursing-care plans up to date. Shoddy-looking areas will be painted. In residential institutions, menus may change a bit and windows will be washed. Vacations may be arranged for certain people during the time the evaluation team is present. Before outside evaluators arrive, you will be told to behave openly and honestly with them. At times, these "inspectors" interview clients. It will be interesting for you to see how clients are chosen for this audience.

In-Service Training

There are three major types of in-service training programs. The traditional in-service day is found in all public schools. The "day" may consist of as many as five days sprinkled throughout the year. They are as standardized as the appearance of an elementary school classroom with the carefully lettered alphabet strung out above the green chalkboards flanked by bulletin boards. For those teachers who haven't made arrangements to play golf or work in their home gardens, the in-service sessions follow a format of introductions that precede a speech by the regional "big boss." One teacher describes the first in-service day of the school term this way:

> The speech always starts out with an interesting and amusing story about little Johnny at school and is usually supplemented by something clever, like "Be a 'FAR' out teacher." The *F* stands for "fair but firm," the *A* for "accountable," and the *R* for "relevant."
>
> After coffee break, which is usually extended for as long as possible, the superintendent of the school region makes his statement. The speech will, of course, evolve around the following words or phrases: "teachers are special people," "sacred obligation," "build better citizens," "concerned individuals," "guiding light of community," "each student is a precious gem, light, popcorn ball," etc., ad infinitum. The speech is concluded with "Let's make this the best year of our educational career."

Mental-health agencies and social-welfare agencies have changed this traditional structure somewhat; they refer to in-service days as *regional conferences.* These conferences are held at large restaurants. Instead of textbook publishers' displays at the teacher workshops, new and innovative programs are described by a long series of speakers. The greatest benefit that staff members can derive from these conferences is a chance to get to see coworkers in a setting outside the agency. Perhaps more important is the opportunity to become acquainted with someone who may be a future referral resource for clients.

The second type of in-service training is run by outsiders—for example, an extension class taught by a professor from a local university, or an expert working with staff members on a specific problem. The value of this type of in-service training depends completely on the quality of the teachers and on the staff who are the students. Some organizations even allow and encourage staff members to take advantage of such training on company time.

The third type of in-service training takes place outside the organization. Many help-giving agencies are encouraging staff members to obtain additional education; in some cases, the agency pays the tuition. Read the fine print when you accept tuition money from your agency. How much do you have to repay if you quit before a certain period of time? An additional caution: education, like many other time-honored institutions, has been affected by the profit motive. There are literally hundreds of educational institutions operating as profit-making enterprises and using the lure of college credit for "life experiences" as a marketing strategy. Some of these institutions have exceptionally high standards; others are diploma mills. Be sure you know the difference before you spend time and money.

The professional conference is another form of outside education. You should attend at least one such conference. You will be amazed to see how people behave away from home. Alcohol becomes the focus of much activity. Casual sex in the rented rooms is not uncommon.

Job-Related Sex

The last section in this chapter deals with the influences of the rush to the future on human-service organizations. As a result of this rush, many people treat sex very casually. Many sad situations could be cited as examples here, but two will suffice.

> I have a friend—a good friend—who's been married for four years. One of the coaches, the same one who approached me time and time again, approached her. Well, she was having problems. This was her first year teaching, and she was impressed with his flattery and enthusiasms. She had an affair with the man. The three of us were free during the same hour, and I sat back, and I watched things: the girl running to get dressed up after a class, making sure that her makeup was fine and her hair combed. The affair is going on now. She has left her husband. What people do is fine, but in school you *do* set an example. The kids see this so much.

A parallel incident that occurred in one agency could have happened anywhere:

> The secretary would always come in late [Thursday] and have to put on her makeup and everything once she got there. I guess Wednesday night is her night out with this guy. People had caught them in different rooms together and stuff like that. Once, there was a big fight over it, like right there when his wife came down— I mean really a wild type thing.

Casual sex between staff members and clients is potentially dangerous. In residential custodial institutions, there is a special problem for staff members who don't have their heads together. It is not unusual for clients who feel confused and powerless to try seduction as a means of obtaining special treatment. To accept their sexual offers is not only unethical but damaging to the institution and to your occupational effectiveness and future career. One specific case will illustrate this point:

> A young female employee has been having sexual relations with a patient on the ward. It has become so obvious, because the employee comes in on her days off to visit the patient. I mean, everybody has started wondering about it. It's so obvious. Here is somebody balling a client. How can she refuse if the client wants to have illegal visitors on the ward or make illegal telephone calls? It's gotten to a situation that's really ridiculous. Now we have started getting dope on the ward, and they can't figure out how.

Often, people who are searching for the answer to "Who am I?" and have the feeling that they may not be quite good enough use sexual activity to take the place of other achievements. Apparently, many healthy and competent people try to boost their egos through a series of sexual encounters. Moreover, many lonely adults try to use sex to take the place of love. If you become involved with either of these two types of people, perhaps you, as one of their partners, might benefit by taking a look at your own needs and motives.

Bureaucratic Celebrations and Sympathy

Office Christmas parties, annual staff picnics, and parties at the boss's home can be fun and interesting. Meeting your coworkers' spouses, friends, and children can give you a new appreciation of the staff. However, these events are always a bit uncomfortable, especially for those who aren't members of the staff. You try to tell them about everybody who will be there before you go, and they try to remember names and act polite, but neither of you really choose to spend time with this group. It's an obligation that you have. Even if the event is for staff members only, they may not be people you would choose for recreation. These events usually are planned by an informal committee, headed by the same people year after year. Before you try to change any aspects of these functions, take a look at the relevant norms. Does everybody draw names at Christmas? Does every staff member give the boss a present?

The memo reading "Those who have not contributed $2 to the flower fund please do so by Friday" is a crude means of expressing sympathy to a coworker during a time of sadness or sickness. Death and illness make us all feel—even for those we don't especially like. In a large group, not all members want to or are able to send a $20 spray to the funeral. Your organization most likely has developed a procedure whereby each staff member contributes a certain amount. Usually, someone in the organization accepts the job of arranging such giving, collecting, and ordering to get the expression of sympathy to the right place at the right time.

Changes in Staff Members

You may not be the only discontented staff member in your organization. Others are trying to change and grow in their own ways. All are trying to reduce the "emotional noise" with which they have to live. Each of us has a private world that we don't often share with others. By sharing the portion of your private world that is associated with your job, you may help your coworkers to share their private job-related thoughts with you. Like all other social exchanges, such sharing will be done selectively. Levels of trust will be tested. Two people can form the beginning of a psychological support system. The job-related support system can be enlarged to include staff members whose concerns are similar. Such an informal group may be used to test ideas and share frustrations. A glimpse into a portion of two changing private worlds might give you some clues as to what might be going on in the heads of some of your coworkers. One teacher had this to share:

> I've really reached the conclusion after just two years that I'm not going to change the system. It will be changed, and I will gladly be a part of that change whenever we clean house. But one thing I do care about is those kids, and if something's not working and they're just hating coming to that class, I try to change it. I survived, and, going to my third year, I can see where I'm going to have much more freedom. I'm going to say "Hey, look. This is the way I feel." And, as of right now, I really don't care if other teachers want to say "What does she think she's doing? Trying to be assistant principal, or is she bucking for a new job, or does she want an increase in pay?" I feel that's their problem, not mine.

A man who had been a prison guard for eight years describes the change that he went through. If you had been working with him, it might have been difficult to believe what you saw. He describes it this way:

> From the time I started, I had been punitive oriented. I believed that you must restrain men, teach them a lesson, punish them for violation of rules and regulations, and keep constant and strict security regulations within the institution. However, I began to wonder about some of these things, and I wondered if they were really necessary to the degree that they were being used.
>
> About this same time, we had a change in wardens and a change in philosophy in the department. I started to attend _____ State University to answer some of the questions that I had about human behavior. Before, I would average close to 4 to 5 tickets a day. This has dropped off. I have found myself able to talk with inmates and get more done than by threatening them or writing a ticket. I found that, within six months, my name as a ticket writer had been dropped. I found that inmates were willing to come up and talk with me about their problems.

Feelings of Failure

When you plunge in full steam ahead with all dedication and no realism, you set yourself up to fail. Go slowly. When you're not sensitive to your own emotions and needs, it's impossible to see clients clearly. Even when you are "together" and think you know what is happening, you will be "taken" in ways that you don't understand. You will feel used, conned, or hustled. Somewhere, you learned that it was wrong to let clients use you—to let them get by with something. When it happens (and it will), the event could lead to the unhappy ending of a relationship. You could see all that you've tried to do as a waste of time; however, there is another way to look at it. The event may be made therapeutic. A real-life example of this kind can be used as a place to really begin helping. It can become a critical incident. It can make your expectations regarding clients more realistic. By confronting clients, you can help them to be more honest with you.

No matter how much you care, show concern, or even love, students will quit, inmates will mess up, patients will die, depressives will commit suicide, and parolees will violate the conditions of their paroles. It's natural to feel that a portion of the failure is your responsibility. Maybe you really did the best you could. If you had it to do over again, perhaps you would do some things differently. Perhaps that will help you with the next challenge. Failure is especially hard on the new staff member who is fired up with humanitarian zeal to help, to give, and to serve. Your own well-being and sanity may be at stake if you accept more than your portion of any failures. More often, after the situation cools off, you'll find out that none of the failure was yours.

Don't Lose Your Keys

As professional helpers, we enter clients' private worlds. We invade their privacy, sometimes to the extreme of stripping them of clothes, cutting their hair, examining their bodily openings, and assigning them numbers in place of their names. Psychoanalysis, therapy, counseling, interviewing, and record keeping may be commonplace to you, but not to the clients. Their privacy becomes public record to you and others. Our society, with its government agencies and computers, is challenging privacy. We all need to hang on to our own private worlds. We need privacy, and we try to protect it. At times, the protection is more symbolic than real; more fragile than strong.

Drawn curtains, glass windows, 4-foot-high office dividers, and sheer clothing provide little real protection of our privacy; they are symbolic dividing lines between what is us and ours and what is others' and public. At the other extreme are elaborate electronic security systems. The most common means of protecting privacy is a lock, but locks also can be used to take away privacy. It is not the lock that provides privacy; it is the key to the lock (Manning, 1972).

The importance of locks and keys ranges from privacy in the family bathroom to arming a thermonuclear weapon. Bureaucratic organizations value locks and keys. They follow complicated procedures in distributing keys, keeping track of who has what keys, and "punishing" those who lose their keys. You will be able to determine who has the most status in your organization, because his or her key will open the most locks—this person may even have a master key. There are at least two exceptions to this rule: (1) the janitor may have a master key, and (2) the boss may not carry a key. Most likely, your keys open doors only in those areas of the institution that are relevant to your job.

What happens when you lose your keys? I lost the keys that were issued to me by the university and was interviewed by a security officer. "Where did you lose them?" "Well, if I knew, I would find them." "When did you lose them?" "I'm not really sure. Sometime between when I had them and now." "Did you look for them? Who helped you look? Did you tell them what the keys opened? Do they work for the university?" After about 40 minutes, I was told that, within the next week, I could come back to the security office and pick up a duplicate set of keys, if my supervisor approved. I had to pay $2 for each lost key.

If you lose a metallic key, the locks can be changed to maintain physical security. At times, we treat the keys to our mental health as though they were the $2 variety. It's only when we start to lose these mental-health keys that we realize their value. Help givers are poor help takers. Helping other people can be an exhausting job, both physically and mentally. Treat the keys to your mental health with care. If you misplace them, ask for help in your search. Although you might be able to find the lost keys without help, the longer you search privately, the harder it will be to remember what your keys looked like.

A Look at the Future

We are rushing into the future. Apparently, nothing can stop the technological rampage. During the 1970s the United States enacted a nation-wide 55-mile speed limit; however, traffic would all but halt on the interstate system if all violators were arrested. We are in a hurry. Each generation has its excuse for the headlong rush (Chickering, 1967).

Domestic social problems of the future are rushing toward us at an even faster rate—they had a head start. Many of our cities are the scene of riots, internally rotten public schools, affluent new industries with tax breaks, and increasing populations of poor Black, White, and Hispanic peoples. Typically, people change careers three times during their lives. This rate will increase. Marriage and divorce rates will become equal. More children will be raised by single parents. Unemployment will climb to a "normal" 10%. Crime rates will continue to climb.

Families move on the average of once every four years. This rate will increase. People are on the move. Addresses will become more temporary. Even now, we are referred to as *occupant* or *resident* by bulk-mail advertisers. The security of a home is being replaced by appliances, furniture, and household gadgets that can be moved from address to address. More children are being cared for by nonrelatives, because parents don't live near the rest of the family. Children's toys are temporary, with their nonreplaceable plastic parts.

Nostalgia is a reflection of our longing for the way things used to be. Some people try to recapture the security of the past by collecting, using, and even wearing relics and other symbols of past eras, but their security is only symbolic.

As people move through temporary relationships, predictable social games become especially important. These games, ranging from simple rituals to complex life games, are poor substitutes for deep human relationships. Since social games are predictable, they provide some continuity as people move from place to place; however, even the most skillful game players sense the meaninglessness as they move from one encounter to the next.

As transients, we will be constantly uprooted from our psychological support systems such as the corner bar, the bridge club, the apartment swimming pool, or the lunch-time gang. As we leave each place, we intend to keep in touch, but we won't. We will move on and try to find substitutes for what we have left behind. Others will take our place; we will take somebody else's place. People are rapidly becoming interchangeable, much like the parts in Eli Whitney's mass-produced rifles. These trends, which Alvin Toffler (1970) labels "future shock" and Erikson (1977) defines as a "chronic disaster," threaten the satisfaction of some of our most basic human needs. The trends are beginning to produce a crushing demand on human services.

Large bureaucratic organizations will crumble. Multiple goals, combined with increasing attempts to reach out for larger budgets while protecting turf, will lead to legal battles between agencies for decreasing tax dollars. Lawyers and legal ritual will provide coherence and form within a disorderly, chaotic system. In the mid-1970s, federal courts were beginning to direct correctional institutions in the United States. The trend toward treating human problems with legal solutions is being accelerated. State mental-health agencies are employing lawyers to protect their patients' rights.

Planning and coordination will be short-term and in response to crises. Titles such as *boundary-spanning personnel* and *ombudsman* will become vogue. Some large organizations are decentralizing into smaller units in order to provide "total service to a region," rather than state-wide service. Some urban-area agencies and organizations are banding together to provide information and referral services in an attempt to meet increasing demand. Like the disposable lighter and modern marriage, these strategies are only temporary.

Consumer demand is beginning to have a real impact on human services. The melting-pot concept is being shattered, as groups assert their distinctive interests within the context of racial, ethnic, class, and sexual identities (Isaacs, 1975). Each group wants culturally compatible staff in human-service organizations. Their demands are supported by the differences that exist between groups in life-styles, values, emotional expressiveness, communication patterns, and family structures. An example of such differences was demonstrated to millions with the first television presentation of *Roots* in January, 1977.

In the near future, we will see "shopping centers" of health, welfare, and educational services, where clients purchase service with a form of script. At the end of each year, agencies will cash in the scripts they have collected for next year's budget. Those agencies that provide the best services to clients—as judged by the number of client scripts collected—will be granted the largest budget. The movement has already begun in state colleges and universities. Budgets are often based on credit-hour production—how many students enroll, and how many classes they *pass.* The competition for clients is especially fierce when the government pays inflated tuition. The competition ranges from matchbook advertising of "GI-Bill approved" to "off campus" graduate-level university programs that employ marketing specialists. These university "salespeople" find themselves thousands of miles from the home campus competing with other universities to recruit classes of service people whose tuition is paid by the federal government.

Profit-making businesses are contracting with school boards to teach children how to read; they offer a money-back guarantee. The presence of alternative schools will cut increasingly into the "average daily attendance" that most states use to allocate funds to the public schools. The same trend is evident *within* some agencies, such as mental health and corrections. The budgets of public mental hospitals are being reduced, largely because the community placement programs have the clients. Parole and probation budgets are increasing at the expense of maintaining and staffing institutions. The competition for clients will increase dramatically if national health insurance or guaranteed annual income becomes law.

Helping, in its various forms, is becoming less professional. There are at least two reasons for this. First, colleges and universities, where most of the helpers are trained, have lowered traditional academic standards in their competition for students. Second, the skills and competencies that are needed in human services are only slightly related to education as we now know it.

"Primary prevention" is becoming a popular phrase. Stop the problems upstream with little dams, so that we don't get a flood in the courts and hospitals. In our primary-prevention work, we have begun (and will continue) to expand programs such as foster-parent training, street therapy, community prevention of mental illness, early-age tutoring, preschool training for handicapped children, and training for infant stimulators. All such programs require staff people who have much more than a formal education.

The effective helpers of tomorrow—including administrators—will need to be recruited and hired on the basis of something more relevant than looks, degrees, and grades. Compared with those who now work in the typical bureaucratic organization, effective staff members of the future will need to be more creative, spontaneous, independent, and self-directed. Traditionally, schools have not encouraged the development of these traits in their students.

Forecasting and preparing for the future costs money. If your organization can barely support its basic services to clients, don't expect much planning. Maybe you will be the one who assumes leadership and changes this situation. In the meantime, enjoy the good feeling you get from a mute's smile, a student's achievement, a parolee's job, a runaway's telephone call, an inmate's early release, or a patient's health. After all, maybe you had something to do with it.

Summary

Don't lose your keys. The organization has loaned you metallic keys that open locks; it creates quite a problem if you lose them. The keys to your mental health are even more important. Many people occasionally experience feelings of failure. Help givers usually are poor help takers.

References

Chickering, S. B. How we got that way. *American Scholar*, 1967, *36*.

Erikson, E. Living in a world without stable points of reference. *World Issues*, Center for the Study of Democratic Institutions, December 1976/January 1977, pp. 13–14.

Isaacs, H. *Idols of the tribe: Group identity and political change.* New York: Harper & Row, 1975.

Kolstoe, O. *College professoring: or Through academia with gun and camera.* Carbondale and Edwardsville: Southern Illinois University Press, 1975.

Manning, P. K. Locks and keys: An essay on privacy. In J. M. Henslin (Ed.), *Down to earth sociology.* New York: Free Press, 1972.

Toffler, A. *Future shock.* New York: Random House, 1970.

Index